W9-DAX-527

Edgar Allan Poe

WHO
WROTE
THAT?

Edgar Allan Poe

Jennifer Peltak

Foreword by
Kyle Zimmer

Chelsea House Publishers
Philadelphia

CHELSEA HOUSE PUBLISHERS

EDITOR IN CHIEF Sally Cheney
DIRECTOR OF PRODUCTION Kim Shinners
CREATIVE MANAGER Takeshi Takahashi
MANUFACTURING MANAGER Diann Grasse

STAFF FOR EDGAR ALLAN POE

ASSOCIATE EDITOR Benjamin Kim
PICTURE RESEARCHER Pat Holl
PRODUCTION EDITOR Megan Emery
SERIES DESIGNER Keith Trego
LAYOUT 21st Century Publishing and Communications, Inc.

http://www.chelseahouse.com

First Printing

1 3 5 7 9 8 6 4 2

Library of Congress Cataloging-in-Publication Data

Peltak, Jennifer.
  Edgar Allan Poe / by Jennifer Peltak.
    p. cm. — (Who wrote that?)
Contents: Once upon a midnight dreary? — The humane heart — I am
dying, yet shall I live — In the greenest of our valleys — Dearest my life is
thine — Out of space, out of time — In sunshine and in shadow.

  ISBN 0-7910-7622-9
  1. Poe, Edgar Allan, 1809-1849—Juvenile literature. 2. Authors,
American—19th century—Biography—Juvenile literature. [1. Poe, Edgar
Allan, 1809-1849. 2. Authors, American.] I. Title. II. Series.
  PS2631.P45 2003
  818'.309—dc22

                                                        2003013687

Table of Contents

FOREWORD BY
KYLE ZIMMER
PRESIDENT, FIRST BOOK

HUMANITY IS POWERED by stories. From our earliest days as thinking beings, we employed every available tool to tell each other stories. We danced, drew pictures on the walls of our caves, spoke, and sang. All of this extraordinary effort was designed to entertain, recount the news of the day, explain natural occurrences—and then gradually to build religious and cultural traditions and establish the common bonds and continuity that eventually formed civilizations. Stories are the most powerful force in the universe; they are the primary element that has distinguished our evolutionary path.

Our love of the story has not diminished with time. Enormous segments of societies are devoted to the art of storytelling. Book sales in the United States alone topped $26 billion last year; movie studios spend fortunes to create and promote stories; and the news industry is more pervasive in its presence than ever before.

There is no mystery to our fascination. Great stories are magic. They can introduce us to new cultures, or remind us of the nobility and failures of our own, inspire us to greatness or scare us to death, but above all, stories provide human insight on a level that is unavailable through any other source. In fact, stories connect each of us to the rest of humanity not just in our own time, but also throughout history.

This special magic of books is the greatest treasure that we can hand down from generation to generation. In fact, that spark in a child that comes from books became the motivation for the creation of my organization, First Book, a national literacy program with a simple mission: to provide new books to the most disadvantaged children. At present, First Book has been at work in hundreds of communities for over a decade. Every year children in need receive millions of books through our organization and millions more are provided through dedicated literacy institutions across the United States and around the world. In addition, groups of people dedicate themselves tirelessly to working with children to share reading and stories in every imaginable setting from schools to the streets. Of course, this Herculean effort serves many important goals. Literacy translates to productivity and employability in life and many other valid and even essential elements. But at the heart of this movement are people who love stories, love to read and want desperately to ensure that no one misses the wonderful possibilities that reading provides.

When thinking about the importance of books, there is an overwhelming urge to cite the literary devotion of great minds. Some have written of the magnitude of the importance of literature. Amy Lowell, an American poet, captured the concept with her statement when she said, "Books are more than books. They are the life, the very heart and core of ages past, the reason why men lived and worked and died, the essence and quintessence of their lives." Others have spoken of their personal obsession with books, as in Thomas Jefferson's simple statement: "I live for books." But more compelling, perhaps, is the almost instinctive excitement in children for books and stories.

Throughout my years at First Book, I have heard truly extraordinary stories about the power of books in the lives of children. In one case, a homeless child, who had been bounced from one location to another, later resurfaced—and the only possession that he had fought to keep was the book he was given as part of a First Book distribution months earlier. More recently, I met a child who, upon receiving the book he wanted, flashed a big smile and said, "This is my big chance!" These snapshots reveal the true power of books and stories to give hope and change lives.

As these children grow up and continue to develop their love of reading, they will owe a profound debt to those volunteers who reached out to them—a debt that they may repay by reaching out to spark the next generation of readers. But there is a greater debt owed by all of us—a debt to the storytellers, the authors, who have bound us together, inspired our leaders, fueled our civilizations, and helped us put our children to sleep with their heads full of images and ideas.

WHO WROTE THAT? is a series of books dedicated to introducing us to a few of these incredible individuals. While we have almost always honored stories, we have not uniformly honored storytellers. In fact, some of the most important authors have toiled in complete obscurity throughout their lives or have been openly persecuted for the uncomfortable truths that they have laid before us. When confronted with the magnitude of their written work or perhaps the daily grind of our own, we can forget that writers are people. They struggle through the same daily indignities and dental appointments, and they experience the intense joy and bottomless despair that many of us do. Yet somehow they rise above it all to deliver a powerful thread that connects us all. It is a rare honor to have the opportunity that these books provide to share the lives of these extraordinary people. Enjoy.

Edgar Allan Poe has become one of modern literature's most beloved and influential figures. "The Raven" has become a contemporary classic, and Poe's legendary (and sometimes wildly exaggerated) life has taken on mythical proportions.

1

"Once Upon a Midnight Dreary"

IN "THE RAVEN," Edgar Allan Poe's famous ode to loss and fear, the narrator struggles to understand why a "ghastly, gaunt, and ominous" black raven has perched, unmoving, above the door to his library. He repeatedly asks the raven its purpose, to which the raven will only mysteriously reply, "Nevermore." As the narrator's anxiety and uncertainty grow, he fears that the bird carries a demonic message. In a panic, he asks the raven impossible questions about his lost love, Lenore, and whether he will be reunited with her in heaven, to which the bird again replies, "Nevermore." At the end of the poem, the maddened narrator reveals that the raven remains in his library and that he can never be free of its torment:

> And my soul from out that shadow that lies floating on the floor
>   Shall be lifted—nevermore!

More than 150 years after Poe penned his gloomy masterpiece, "The Raven" remains a beloved work of art. Tributes to it are so numerous that any reference to a raven easily summons images of *the* Raven. "Nevermore," the raven's chilling one-word message, is instantly recognizable even outside the context of the poem. The line that precedes it, "Quoth the raven," also keeps a permanent perch in the American lexicon.

"The Raven," as Richard Kopley and Kevin J. Hayes observed, "is stamped with the image of true genius— and genius in its happiest hour." Why does a poem about a man driven insane by a bird continue to resonate with generation after generation of readers? The answer lies in Poe's talent and his ability to give his audience an "alluring mix of accessibility and mystery." The poem opens with a moment nearly everyone experiences, that of being awake late at night and hearing a strange noise. In this case, a "rapping, rapping at my chamber door." What happens next has since become a familiar staple of horror movies. The odd, unidentifiable sounds continue and the narrator's anxiety increases even after he flings open his library door to find "darkness there and nothing more."

When the narrator closes the door, the tapping resumes, this time outside his window. He opens the window and a "stately" raven flies in. Once the raven has spoken his ominous line, Poe introduces what he described in one of his short stories as "Horror the soul of the plot." The narrator admits that he seeks peace from the memory of Lenore—"I had sought from my books a surcease of sorrow"—while praising her as a "rare and radiant maiden." The raven provides no explanation about his presence, but the tortured narrator believes it must be about Lenore. He asks the raven if his soul shall ever again "Clasp a rare and radiant maiden whom the angels name Lenore." The steady reply of "Nevermore" haunts the narrator, who is unable to reconcile the loss of Lenore. That loss is the heart of the poem. Despite the element of horror and fantasy, "The Raven" is, according to Kopley and Hayes, ultimately "a poem about remembering."

The continued popularity of "The Raven" cannot be explained entirely by Poe's gift for language and story-telling. Like the grief-stricken characters in his stories and poems, Poe suffered much tragedy and loss before his death. His mother died, possibly of yellow fever, when Poe was two, and his father had disappeared the previous year. Poe was raised away from his brother and sister, and the relationship he reestablished with his brother in early adulthood was cut short by his brother's sudden death. During adolescence, a beloved female family friend died, and Poe's foster mother also died at an early age a few years later. The close relationship with his foster father turned strained and bitter as Poe grew older, and they eventually stopped speaking. Poe's earliest romance was cut short when the girl's family refused to let them see each other. When "The Raven" was published in early 1845, Poe's young wife, Virginia Clemm, had been wasting away from tuberculosis for three years.

Poe's misfortunes were not limited to his relationships.

He spent his life trying to rise above poverty with little success. He was desperate for fame and praise, which he achieved—along with a long list of enemies and detractors. Like his father and brother, Poe had a lifelong drinking problem that played an important part in his mysterious death. His friends and acquaintances described him as a man who often appeared haunted and sad. Several photos of Poe survive and continue to be reprinted on postcards, advertisements, and posters. They mostly portray a dark, sad-eyed man with a grave face, no doubt contributing to the Poe mystique.

Yet Poe's reputation for investigating the dark corners of the soul extends far beyond the horrors of "The Raven." In "The Fall of the House of Usher," perhaps Poe's most famous short story, the narrator visits a childhood friend, Roderick Usher, who has fallen ill along with his sister, Madeline. After Madeline dies, the narrator becomes increasingly anxious over Roderick's growing madness and his own indescribable fear, which he can only attribute to the ghostly family mansion. As a storm rages one night, Roderick admits to burying his sister alive. At that moment, Madeline reappears and Roderick dies of fright. As the narrator races out of the mansion, the House of Usher collapses behind him.

In another famous Poe tale, "The Tell-Tale Heart," the narrator murders the man he lives with and hides his corpse beneath the floorboards. He believes he has gotten away with his crime until he begins hearing the heartbeat of the dead man. Unable to bear the deafening sound, he confesses to the police. Gruesome situations are the normal landscape of Poe's tales. In "The Cask of Amontillado," the narrator walls up an acquaintance while he is still alive, never explaining his motives. "The

Pit and the Pendulum" finds the narrator trapped in a dark hole surrounded by instruments of torture and death by captors he cannot see.

Characters who believe they can treat others cruelly or cheat death are punished in Poe's stories for their arrogance. The partygoers in "The Masque of Red Death" seal themselves up in a castle to escape the plague sweeping the land. There, they hold decadent costume parties until Death himself arrives as a masked guest. In "Hop-Frog," a deformed court jester punishes his abusive king by setting him and his court on fire.

If Poe's poems are somewhat less terrifying, they are often equally as grim. In poems such as "The Raven," "Lenore," "Ulalume" and "Annabel Lee," the narrators lament their lost loves, who are often idealized as youthful, beautiful, and perfect maidens. Several of the women in Poe's life died in their youth, including his wife from tuberculosis. The physical signs of tuberculosis include pale, luminous skin, and red cheeks. As the victims slowly faded away, they sometimes appeared attractive and healthy. Poe captured this irony in "The Masque of Red Death" by hiding Death in a magnificent costume. According to Hayes, Poe addressed the wasted beauty he witnessed in his wife and other women by populating his stories and poems with "gentle, vulnerable, delicate females" with fair hair and large, luminous eyes. Critics have suggested that Poe raises the dead so believably in his fiction because it was such a constant fact of his life.

The dead characters in Poe's tales and poems rarely stay that way. They might seek revenge for being buried alive. In stories such as "The Tell-Tale Heart" and "Ligeia," the deceased return to torture the living. Poe chose to leave unclear whether his characters are confronting an actual ghost, or rather, manifestations of a guilt and loss that are driving them insane. In "Ligeia," after the title character dies, her husband remarries a woman who also falls ill and appears to die. As the narrator watches, the corpse appears to come alive on her deathbed and then die again, each time becoming increasingly beautiful in life and horrific in death. When the narrator finally summons the nerve to remove his wife's death shroud, he finds it is Ligeia, who has possessed his second wife's body.

It is Poe's thrilling and macabre tales, along with the bleak facts of his life, which have contributed to his enduring image as, according to critic Mark Neimeyer,

Did you know...

Poe's "grave and stern" bird has been used to name a beer, a professional football team, restaurants, and art galleries. The poem has been drawn and painted countless times, including an illustration by impressionist painter Edward Manet. Horror movie legend Bela Lugosi filmed a version of "The Raven" in 1935, and Oscar-winning actor Jack Nicholson starred in a 1963 adaptation of the poem. The popular, long-running television cartoon series *The Simpsons* dramatized "The Raven" for one of its Halloween episodes, and used "The Tell-Tale Heart" for another episode. The U.S. Navy even christened one of its minesweepers the *U.S.S. Raven*.

"the archetype of the mad genius or the tortured romantic artist . . . crushed by a crass and insensitive world." His name today is nearly synonymous with melancholy and despair. Poe's unsavory reputation, prominent during his life, has flourished since his death in 1849. Yet much of what is assumed about Poe is not true, or is exaggerated. Poe himself was not always accurate about the facts of his life. He wrote biographical essays boasting about accomplishments that never took place, such as heading his class at West Point. In reality, Poe was discharged.

Throughout his career as a magazine writer, Poe created hoaxes and outright fabrications. After moving to New York City in 1844, for instance, he sold a made-up story to a newspaper claiming to have crossed the Atlantic Ocean in three days in a hot-air balloon. Clearly, Poe did not limit his imagination to fiction. It was not Poe, however, who created the myth of Poe as the dissolute madman that persists today. Less than a year after his death, Rufus Griswold published the first Poe biography. Unfortunately, Griswold, who had maintained an uneasy relationship with Poe while he was alive, decided in death to slander him. His book, the only Poe biography for several decades, cemented the Poe legend through its distorted facts.

Although numerous biographers since Griswold have reported the facts of Poe's life, a smeared reputation is not an easy thing to fix. Even today, according to Hayes, "his problems with alcohol have frequently been exaggerated, and his one documented use of laudanum [an opium derivative] has . . . been transformed into a lifelong opium habit. Poe's marriage, at twenty-six, to his thirteen-year-old cousin, Virginia, is rarely mentioned without suggesting some sort of deviant sexuality, and the mysterious circumstances surrounding his death have been the source of endless . . . speculation."

A poster available at the Poe Museum in Richmond, Virginia—where Poe grew up—summarizes the contradiction within the myths: "Sadomasochist, drug addict, manic depressive, pervert, egomaniac, alcoholic? When did Poe find time to write?" Poe was, in fact, a hardworking artist. That he created a body of genius despite hardships and poverty indicates a man dedicated to his art. Evidence of the "consummate craftsman" can be found in his construction of "The Raven." According to Hayes, Poe's rhyme scheme "is consistently ABCBBB and . . . he occasionally offered a rippling internal rhyme— 'dreary,' 'weary'; 'napping,' 'tapping'; 'uttered,' 'fluttered.' His use of alliteration is compelling, effectively contributing to the lulling, incantatory quality of the language." Poe drew the reader in with his tight composition, "intensifying the effect with a limited physical space and the progression of the [narrator's] questions."

Poe outlined his theories about writing in several important essays. In "The Philosophy of Composition," he asserted that poems ought "to be readable at a single sitting, and . . . work to elevate the soul of the reader." Poe believed that a beautiful work of art should be the result of careful calculations. He also aimed "to redirect critical attention onto technique, to art as a clever allusion which the artist controls . . . ."

One of his great achievements, in fact, was his invention of the detective genre with "The Murders in the Rue Morgue." Detective stories of course rely heavily on their heroes' powers of logic and calculation. According to Kenneth Silverman, Poe depicted in detective Auguste Dupin, "his mental processes in solving mysterious crimes

Horror movie legend Bela Lugosi made a film called The Raven *in 1935. In it, he plays a doctor who is obsessed with Edgar Allan Poe, and fellow actor Boris Karloff (known for his title roles in many Frankenstein movies) is the doctor's servant. Clearly, Poe's fame had permeated popular culture even in the early twentieth century.*

. . . [as differing] little from the kind of thinking by which Poe had often before made the impossible possible." Poe is also widely viewed as a pioneer of science fiction. His interest in hoaxes and the fantastic, as well as the machinery of the industrial age, led to stories such as "The Unparalleled Adventures of One Hans Pfaall," a story of moon travel.

Readers of Poe enjoy his stories and poems because his careful construction and precise writing elevates their apprehension and fear. Poe owes his enduring popularity, however, to what he wrote, not how he wrote it. Like his ghastly raven, Poe's place in American culture is secure, and his image instantly recognizable. His poems have been recited in John Wayne movies, and the Beatles put his face on one of their albums. There are Poe stamps and alarm clocks. The Mystery Writers of America call their annual awards the Edgars, and the popular book series, *The Idiot's Guide*, features Poe on the cover of its literature guide as the only illustration. Both Baltimore and Richmond claim Poe as a native son, and Philadelphia, New York City, and Boston all maintain historical sites dedicated to Poe. His books have been translated into nearly every language. There have been special editions designed for children as well as comic books aimed at all age groups.

Poe wrote his stories and poems with the aim of reaching the popular market. His popularity endures into the twenty-first century because of his skillful ability to frighten and disturb. In the 150 years since Poe's death, there has been an American civil war, two world wars, and the invention of the atomic bomb. Sigmund Freud's theories on the actions of the unconscious mind would not have seemed out of place in Poe's stories. Horror movies attract huge audiences eager to be scared and surprised. If anything, Poe's stories are more modern than when they were first written. If his status as a great writer has not always been sure, Patrick Quinn writes that "today his fame is secure. The America in which he could find no adequate reward treasures every word he wrote, and in every city in which he lived . . . stands a memorial to him."

Poe's English-born mother, actress Elizabeth Arnold, had acted since she was a child, even appearing onstage in America at age nine. Her death at the age twenty-four would have a great effect on young Poe, and he was separated from his siblings and cared for by John and Frances Allan.

2

The Humane Heart

EDGAR ALLAN POE was born Edgar Poe on January 19, 1809, the second son of two traveling actors. Before he was old enough to write, Edgar had experienced tragedy and loss that would forever haunt him, laying the groundwork for his remarkable but troubled career.

Poe's mother, Elizabeth Arnold, was a celebrated actress who spent nearly her entire life moving from town to town, seeking work on the stage. Born in England, she immigrated to Boston in 1796 with her mother, also an actress. The identity and fate of her father is unknown. Just nine years old when she appeared on

American stages, Eliza earned instant praise for her precocious acting abilities. One critic wrote: "Her powers as an actress would do credit to any of her sex of a maturer age." Acting in that time was a grueling occupation. Large sections of the public thought of the theater as "an immoral institution," and looked down upon actors. Actors worked long seasons for low pay and could rarely put stakes down in any town long enough to start a stable existence.

Less than two years after their arrival in the new world, Eliza's mother died of a fever while traveling through North Carolina. Orphaned, Eliza continued acting, the only life she was trained for. Audiences loved the beautiful young girl, and she was emerging as a talented singer and dancer. In order to keep theaters packed and profitable, plays changed often, which meant a busy actor had to keep learning different parts. By fifteen, Eliza had played about seventy different roles. One Philadelphia newspaper suggested that, "in a short time, she will be unequalled in her profession." That same year, Eliza married her first husband. He died three years later, possibly from the same fever that took her mother.

By eighteen, Eliza was an accomplished actress. She was regularly partnered with David Poe, Jr., an actor and dancer from Baltimore three years older than Eliza. Unlike Eliza, he came from a family of some prominence. His father was a Revolutionary War hero, and David had been studying law before he chose to pursue an acting career. Although he was handsome and possessed a deep voice, he had no particular talent for acting. Newspaper reports indicate he suffered from paralyzing stage fright. His acting was dismissed as an "abyss of embarrassment." Despite poor reviews, David continued acting alongside Eliza. They married in the 1806, and the new bride billed herself as Eliza Poe.

Perhaps seeking a more stable home life, the Poes settled

in Boston, where they performed for the next three years, thirty weeks a year. Eliza embraced the city where she debuted as an actress. Her reviews were usually positive, and she began acting in more serious roles such as Juliet in *Romeo and Juliet*. She found time to paint a watercolor of the city's harbor, which later became one of Edgar's cherished possessions. Four months after they moved to Boston, Eliza gave birth to her first son, William. Two years later, in the midst of a violent winter, Edgar Poe was born.

Pregnancy did not put Eliza's career on hold. She continued acting until ten days before Edgar was born and resumed working three weeks after his birth. It is not clear whom Edgar was named for, though it could have been Mr. Edgar, the manager of the troupe Eliza who was working for when her mother died. Edgar's birth and the financial demands of supporting a family strained the young marriage, however. David Poe, continually dogged by poor reviews in Boston, left the theater company not long after Eliza returned to work. He headed to Baltimore, hoping the Poes would give him some assistance. His request for money from a wealthy cousin was turned down.

A few months after Edgar was born, the family moved to New York. While Eliza worked, David sought comfort in alcohol. His drunkenness forced him to drop out of performances, and he and Eliza fought. Just six weeks after they moved to New York, David Poe disappeared, and his wife and children never saw him again. Like his youngest son, the end of David Poe's life is shrouded in mystery. Some reports indicate that "nothing is known of where David went, or of what became of him." Other sources claim that Poe died in Norfolk, Virginia, within the year from some kind of fever. What is certain is that Eliza and her two sons were poor and very much alone. The actress was very well liked by the public and critics, and when her personal loss became known, benefit performances were announced to raise money for "private misfortunes." Within a year of David Poe's disappearance, Eliza gave birth to her last child, a daughter named Rosalie.

Eliza continued acting and touring throughout the South with her young brood. While critics lavished praise on her as "a brilliant gem in the theatric crown," they also noticed something was amiss with the young actress. A reviewer in Norfolk, Virginia, said: "Misfortunes have pressed heavy on her. . . . She no longer commands that admirations and attention as she formerly did." In fact, Eliza had fallen ill. By November 1811, she was bedridden. Her fellow actors staged two benefits for her, and a late November notice in the *Richmond Enquirer* pleaded for the public's assistance:

TO THE HUMANE HEART
> On this night, Mrs. Poe, lingering on the bed of
> disease and surrounded by her children, asks
> your assistance; and asks it perhaps for the last time.

Concerned citizens responded with nurses and cooks. However, Eliza was unable to recover. On December 8, 1811, Eliza Poe died at twenty-four, surrounded by her children. The oldest, William, later recalled that she spoke a final goodbye, and that he was given a lock of her hair after her death. Eliza had few possessions, but Edgar, then nearly three, received her watercolor painting of Boston. On the back she wrote, "For my little son Edgar, who should ever love Boston, the place of his birth, and where his mother found her best, and most sympathetic friends."

The three Poe children were separated. A Richmond family took in Rosalie. David Poe's family had taken in William, but could not afford to care for Edgar. Frances

Poe's foster father John Allan was originally from Scotland. The relationship between Poe and Allan was tempestuous to say the least, and would be marked with confrontation throughout their lives.

Allan was one of the well-to-do ladies of Richmond who visited Eliza on her deathbed, and she took a liking to Edgar. She had no children with her husband, John Allan, a wealthy merchant who sold tobacco and other goods. He resisted Frances' pleas at first, but in a short time John Allan had written to David Poe's family, asking to take the middle child in. Edgar Poe soon joined the Allan household. Although Frances and John Allan gave Edgar their last name, they never adopted him. It was a feeling of being welcomed but not quite accepted that would plague Edgar into adulthood.

Poe's early years with the Allans were happy and highly productive, despite the loss of his parents and separation from William and Rosalie. The tragedies of Poe's life provided the palette from which he created his most profound works. Without the education and initial encouragement he received from his foster parents, however, Poe's skills and intellect might have remained undeveloped.

Poe and John Allan, however, could not have been more different. Allan, a Scottish immigrant, was a successful businessman with much money to lavish on clothes, food, travel, and entertainment. He bought a piano for his house, subscribed to an encyclopedia and quoted authors such as Jonathan Swift and William Shakespeare. Yet one friend described him as "impulsive and quick-tempered . . . rather rough and uncultured." Allan had adopted hard work and self-sacrifice as his formula for success, begrudged the good fortune of others, and despised any hint of laziness. He was fond of bland advice such as, "I always choose to be on the safe side," and "Never fail to your Duty to your Creator first, to your Employer next." His envious comment about Shakespeare—"Gods! What I would not give, if I had his talent for writing!"—suggests that Allan knew his talents did not extend into the arts.

Allan's wife, Frances, by contrast, was "flirtatious and high-spirited" but often bedridden with some unspecified, possibly imaginary illness. With none of her husband's pretensions, she doted on Edgar. The Allans dressed Edgar like "a little prince," as much an ornament as a foster son. At age three, Edgar was described as "a lovely little fellow, with dark curls and brilliant eyes . . . charming every one by his childish grace, vivacity, and cleverness." His gift for poetry and melody was already evident, and the Allans loved to have Edgar entertain their friends. Edgar's "memory and music ear enabled him to learn and recite the most moving and beautiful passages of English poetry. He was encouraged to stand on the dining room table in his stockinged feet and toast the health of the ladies with a glass of sweetened wine."

In 1815, John Allan decided it would be profitable to open an English branch of his Richmond-based business, and so the Allans and six-year-old Edgar moved to London for five years. Here Edgar was introduced to Britain's tradition of rigorous schooling, where the already precocious Poe excelled. His headmaster later recalled that "when he left [the school] he was able to speak the French language, construe any easy Latin author, and was far better acquainted with history and literature than many boys of a more advanced age who had had greater advantages than he had had." John Allan remarked in a letter that, "Edgar is a fine Boy and I have no reason to complain of his progress . . . Edgar is growing wonderfully, & enjoys a good reputation."

Despite his academic progress, Poe had begun suffering from the isolation and loneliness that was to be a fixture of his life. Poe lived in a boarding school, the Manor House School, a few miles outside of London, and the separation from the Allans, especially Fannie, was traumatic for a young boy who had lost his parents only a few years before. Several of Poe's stories contain details from his stay in England, and in "William Wilson" he named the stern headmaster after the head of his boarding school. Poe's narrator describes the school's dreariness, noting, "how little was there to remember!"

Poe's education in England was cut short when an economic crisis drove John Allan deep into debt and forced him to close the London office. The family returned to Richmond where they struggled financially for several years. Edgar was able to continue his education, and his gifts as a writer blossomed. By sixteen, Edgar had assembled enough poems for a book, and he tried to persuade John Allan to fund the publication. Poe's headmaster talked Allan out of it, arguing that Poe was vain and easily flattered, and that publishing the book would only encourage those tendencies.

When Poe returned from England, his education largely exceeded his fellow students. His competitive, driven side was already apparent. Poe's classmates described him as "eager for distinction" and "ambitious to excel." Although later in life Poe would become notable for his pale, ravaged features, as a teenager he was athletic and spry, and as mischievous as any boy his age. One friend recalled that he "liked masquerades, practical jokes and raiding orchards." Thomas Ellis, the son of John Allan's business partner, recalled that Edgar "led me to do many a forbidden thing, for which I was punished." His antics with Ellis were not always entirely successful. Ellis wrote, "I ought to mention that he once saved me from drowning—for having thrown me into the falls headlong, that I might strike out for myself, he presently found it necessary to come to my help or it would have been too late." At age fifteen, Edgar swam six miles against the tide of the James River, his finest moment of athletic prowess, which he would boast about repeatedly throughout his life. Poe compared the feat to "[swimming] twenty miles in still water."

As Poe's education continued, he became a stellar classical scholar, able to read Latin and Greek. Although the somewhat unruly student did not always prepare for class, he was able to fall back on his quick wit and cleverness. The same headmaster who persuaded John Allan that Poe was not ready to become a published author was still quite sensitive to his pupil's gifts. His comments in one report quietly foreshadow the themes Poe would develop as an adult: "His imaginative powers seemed to take precedence of all his other faculties, he gave proof of this, in some of his juvenile compositions addressed to his young female friends. He had a sensitive and tender heart, and would strain every nerve to oblige a friend."

The same year that Edgar displayed his athletic abilities in the James River, he suffered the next major loss of his young life. Jane Stannard was the mother of one of Edgar's friends. When his home life started to fray as he reached adolescence, it was Jane whom Edgar turned to for "comfort and consolation." Little is known about their relationship, according to biographer Arthur Hobson Quinn, except that "she spoke some gracious words of welcome, she was beautiful, and he was in a mood in which a woman's sympathy must have been needed." Less than a year after they met, Jane, who had suffered from depression for years, went insane and died suddenly at twenty-eight. Edgar took the loss very badly, and, along with Jane's son, he often visited her grave at night. He later described Jane in a letter as "the first, purely ideal love of my soul." His tribute to Jane, "To Helen," is considered one of Poe's most beautiful poems. The famous stanza

> To the glory that was Greece
> And the grandeur that was Rome

compared Jane's beauty to a "classical ideal" of beauty.

The loss of Jane Stannard marked a turning point in Edgar's life. He was becoming a moody adolescent, developing a sensitivity to his precarious place in the Allan household. Although John Allan provided for the boy's welfare, both failed to rouse affection in the other. Allan also had a quick temper, and according to biographer Jeffrey Meyers, when he was angry he "threatened to turn him adrift, and that he

Frances "Fanny" Allan, Poe's foster mother, was a very loving and doting parent in contrast to John Allan. She and Poe kept in close touch during Poe's time in the army. Her death in 1829 allowed Poe to reconcile with John Allan if only briefly, easing the way for Poe's entry into West Point the following year.

never allowed him to lose sight of his dependence upon his charity." A letter from John Allan in 1824 documents the growing rift: " . . . [He] does nothing & seems quite miserable, sulky & ill-tempered to all the Family. How we have acted to produce this is beyond my conception—why I have put up so long with his conduct is a little less wonderful."

After Jane Stannard's death, Poe developed his first genuine romance with Elmira Royster, a Richmond neighbor. Though Elmira was only fifteen, the two became secretly engaged. Two and a half decades after Poe's death, Elmira remembered, "He was a beautiful boy—Not very talkative. When he did talk he was pleasant but his general manner was sad." Her recollections also indicate that Poe's passionate nature was already evident: "He had strong prejudices. Hated anything coarse and unrefined. Never spoke of his [real] parents. . . . He was warm and zealous in any cause he was interested in, very enthusiastic and impulsive."

Elmira's father, however, did not approve of Edgar, possibly because of his daughter's youth, but also, as a "poor orphan," Poe was "probably considered unsuitable for social and financial reasons." In fact, her father intercepted the letters Elmira and Poe sent each other while Poe was in his first year of college. Upon his return for Christmas break, he was heartbroken to learn Elmira was engaged to another man.

Poe's two years at the University of Virginia brought his relationship with John Allan to the breaking point. As Poe entered the university in 1826, it was just a year old. Thomas Jefferson oversaw the college he founded and "every Sunday he regularly invited some of the students to dine with him at Monticello." Two other presidents, James Madison and James Monroe, oversaw examinations, including Poe's. Jefferson had high goals for his school, aiming to "develop the reasoning faculties of our youth, enlarge their minds, cultivate their morals, and instill into them the precepts of virtue and order." Jefferson believed his students would follow a system of few rules and self-governance.

However, the former president's system was somewhat less than successful in its early years. A riot erupted during the school's first year, and students "threw bricks and bottles at the professors." Meyers writes that "The wild male code of fighting, sports, drinking and gambling . . . took over." Poe noted, "a common fight is so trifling an occurrence that no notice is taken of it." The rough atmosphere unnerved Edgar, and he reported in letters to John Allan that a number of students carried pistols, and he witnessed one fight that ended with a "savage" biting.

Yet Poe excelled at the Charlottesville school. He studied ancient and modern languages and received some of the highest honors in both. Poe, according to a classmate, "rarely had to prepare his lessons in advance. His intellect and memory were so acute that he required only a few minutes of study before class in order to give the best recitation." Yet the melancholy aspect of Poe's personality deepened at the University of Virginia, and his classmates and teachers gave conflicting reports as they encountered his mood swings. He was remembered as "a pretty wild young man" but also as a "sober, quiet and orderly young man." Another student painted Poe as a complex, difficult figure to capture:

> [Poe] was fond of quoting poetic authors and reading poetic productions of his own, with which his friends were delighted and entertained; then suddenly a change would come over him; he would with a piece of charcoal evince his versatile genius by sketching upon the walls of his dormitory, whimsical, fanciful and grotesque figures, with so much artistic skill, as to leave us in doubt whether Poe in future life would be

Painter or Poet. He was very excitable & restless, at times wayward, melancholic & morose, but again—in his better moods . . . full of fun.

Some of Poe's classmates tellingly noted that his moods were easily excited when "under the invisible spirit of wine." In fact, he began his lifelong battle with alcohol while in college.

He also developed a gambling habit, despite being completely unable to pay his debts. In a moment of crisis, Poe decided that John Allan was the source of his misfortune. Allan had sent Poe to Charlottesville with $110, which, according to Meyers, covered "board and attendance at the two schools. Still owing $15 for room rent, $12 for a bed, and $12 more for furniture . . . he took on debts from the start." Just a week after he started school, Poe wrote to Allan asking for money. Allan sent enough to cover his debts, plus one dollar. Quinn notes, "To a college where . . . the great majority of the young men spent at least five hundred dollars in one session, Poe was sent by John Allan deliberately, without a decent allowance."

Allan invariably responded to Poe's requests for money with a short temper, and Poe became increasingly despondent and bitter over his foster father's behavior. His letters to Allan were, by turn, pleading, hopeful, accusatory, and hostile. In one letter he states: "I will boldly say that it was wholly and entirely your own mistaken parsimony that caused all of the difficulties in which I was involved while at Charlottesville."

At the end of Poe's first year of college, Allan refused to pay for a second term. Upon returning to Richmond, Poe lasted just a few days before he and Allan had an explosive argument, fueled by grievances dating back to the death of Jane Stannard. Poe left the house and moved to a nearby

Thomas Jefferson founded the University of Virginia in 1825, and would invite students to dine with him at his home in Monticello. However, Poe witnessed many fights and riots as well on campus, and wrote to John Allan describing the school's violent atmosphere.

tavern, where he and Allan exchanged bitter letters. Poe believed that Allan had led him to expect a certain financial security, and then ruthlessly cut him off. However, at the core of Poe's complaints was his belief that the Allans had never truly accepted him as a son. Allan, always angered by Poe's petulant ultimatums, refused to help. He also hinted that Poe's obvious talent for writing was a waste of time. Lost and penniless, Poe set sail for Boston (possibly working to pay his passage) in late March 1827. His goal, as a tortured letter to Allan attests, was to "leave your house and endeavor to find some place in this wide world, where I will be treated—not as *you* have treated me."

At least one critic has argued that part of Poe's personal tragedy stemmed from the relative wealth and comfort of his childhood and teenage years, which he was then cast from with little explanation. Meyers writes that he "was carefully reared through the first eighteen years of his life to conform to the manners and code of the aristocratic, landed gentry . . . then he was suddenly thrust into the business world where the only money he ever made came from that otherwise discredited instrument in the world of finance— a writer's pen." Over the next few years Poe would attempt to support himself by any other means besides writing. He tried to continue his education while still seeking support and money from John Allan, but the relationship between the two never recovered and eventually disintegrated entirely.

His family had no idea where Poe had gone. Poe would later claim that he had traveled to Greece to fight for Greek independence, and that he had been to Russia. Reality was less colorful. Upon his arrival in Boston, Poe worked a series of mundane jobs. Frustrated because none provided him the support he needed, on May 26, 1827, Poe enlisted in the U.S. Army for five years as "Edgar A. Perry." Just eighteen, Poe gave his age as twenty-two. Poe's service was unremarkable, although he later set several stories in the places he visited, notably South Carolina in "The Gold Bug."

Boston, the city of Poe's birth, represented another notable moment in Poe's life—the publication of his first book. *Tamerlane and Other Poems* was published anonymously with the credit "By a Bostonian" in July 1827. Poe paid for the 40-page pamphlet himself. No one reviewed it, and the publication went without notice. Ironically, twelve original copies of *Tamerlane* survive, making it one of the most valuable American first editions. Poe asserted in the book's preface that most of the poems were written by the time he was fourteen, though it is unknown whether that is true. The poems are preoccupied with youth and finding a place in the world.

Despite the growing rift between his army career and his personal, literary ambitions, Poe did very well in the army. By 1829, he had risen to sergeant major for artillery, the highest rank for a noncommissioned officer. After two years, Poe had had enough. His commanding officer agreed to let Poe leave the army early only if he mended relations with John Allan. Allan let the commanding officer know he felt Poe was better off in the army. Poe's personal letters to John Allan went unanswered. In his last letter, Poe tried to convince Allan that he should attend West Point. Although Poe at first wished to quit the military, the rigorous academic life at West Point might have appealed to him, as well as the prestige of attending the military school, which would have appealed to Poe's vanity.

Despite the acrimony between Allan and Poe, Poe kept a close relationship with Fanny Allan, who never stopped doting on her foster son. In Poe's army letters to Allan, he repeatedly inquires about Fanny Allan, who had fallen ill.

Did you know...

The French poet Charles Baudelaire, who later translated Poe's works, described Poe's drinking as "savage." His classmates noted that when Poe drank, "it was not the taste of the beverage that influenced him . . . he would seize a full glass, without water or sugar, and send it home with a single gulp." Once intoxicated, Poe was out of control. Never one to do anything halfway, when Poe drank, he always drank to excess, often to the point of illness and total insensibility.

On February 28, 1829, she died at age forty-four. Poe arrived in Richmond the night after Fanny's burial, and her death brought the two grieving men together. They reconciled. Allan now agreed to let Poe leave the army and help him secure an appointment at West Point. However, it was nearly two years before Poe was accepted as a cadet. During that time, he traveled to Baltimore, living with his birth father's family for the first time and scratching out a meager living. His one significant accomplishment was the publication of a second volume of poetry, *Al Aaraaf, Tamerlane and Minor Poems*, in December 1829 by a Baltimore publisher. The title poem was named for the Muslim version of Purgatory, where dead souls are neither happy nor suffering. Though "Al Aaraaf" had some promising moments, it was too reminiscent of Poe's influences, and incomprehensible in other passages. The relative failure of such a lengthy poem convinced Poe that the best poems, "to be effective, must be short."

Poe entered West Point in the summer of 1830. Unlike the University of Virginia, the cadets at West Point were expected to follow a constricted routine, forbidden most pleasures, and expected to live in uncomfortable quarters with terrible food. Poe excelled once again; according to Meyers, "at the end of his first half year he finished, in a class of eighty-seven, third in French and seventeenth in mathematics." Despite the strict routine, Poe continued his furtive writings and alcohol consumption. A classmate described him as having "a worn, weary, discontented look, not easily forgotten by those who were intimate with him."

Matters worsened considerably for Poe that fall when John Allan remarried. An offhand comment Poe had once made to an acquaintance, that Allan was "not very often sober," got back to Allan. It was not true, and he was infuriated. At the

Poe attended West Point (shown here) in 1830 after leaving the army with the help of John Allen's influence. However, after Allen had remarried, his relationship with Poe became even more strained. Poe even threatened to get himself expelled from West Point if Allen would not allow him to leave.

end of 1830, he sent Poe a letter apparently stating that he wanted "no further communication with [Poe]." In the meantime, Poe had decided that he no longer wanted to be at West Point. His decision angered Allan, who had pulled many strings to get his foster son into the school. Hurt and angry over what he perceived as numerous injustices from Allan, Poe launched a war of words. He demanded that Allan give his consent to leave West Point, or Poe would simply have himself kicked out. Allan ignored Poe's demands and asserted to a friend that, "I do not think the Boy has one good quality."

True to his word, Poe elected to get kicked out of West

Point. He neglected nearly all of his classes and duties, and was court-martialed by the academy in late January 1831. Deliberating just one day, the court found Poe guilty on all charges and dismissed him from West Point. In a typical display of Poe's confidence and bravado, he stayed at West Point another month to persuade his former classmates to contribute to the publication of his next book of poems. Poe wrote a final letter to John Allan, once again accusing him of neglect. Allan responded that Poe's letter came from "the Blackest Heart & deepest ingratitude." Yet Allan also paid tribute to his foster son's literary gift while foreshadowing the torment that would accompany it, saying, "Suffice it to say my only regret is in Pity for his failings—his Talents are of an order than can never prove a comfort to their possessor."

Poe traveled to New York City after leaving West Point, and with donations from his classmates, brought out *Poems by Edgar A. Poe* in 1831. Expecting to see satires of West Point life, Poe's classmates were unhappy to see a serious, but cheaply made, volume of poetry. The cadets greeted the volume "with a general expression of disgust." Yet Poe's third book was considered a remarkable achievement for a twenty-two-year-old poet. Some of his most famous poems, including "To Helen," the tribute to Jane Stannard, were included in the volume. According to Meyers, Poe had begun to master his recurring themes of "victimization, power and powerlessness, confrontations with mysterious presences, extreme states of being . . . [and] memory of and mourning for the dead."

After leaving New York, Poe traveled to Baltimore, where he intended to settle among David Poe's relatives. Leaving the gentleman's life in Richmond, Poe entered a much different society. Here, he would pursue the perfection of his craft and the deepest relationships of his life.

When Poe returned to Baltimore, he lived with his aunt, Maria Poe Clemm, and her daughter Virginia. Poe would soon develop romantic feelings toward his cousin, and the two would marry in 1836.

3

I Am Dying,
Yet Shall I Live

IN 1831, EDGAR Allan Poe returned to Baltimore. The city most closely associated with Poe, Baltimore was the one link to his blood relatives. Poe's years in Baltimore, from 1831 to 1834, are the least documented of his life. Out on his own for the first time, he pursued his ambitions, worked hard, and was often saddled with mundane jobs or unemployment. His relationship with John Allan was all but severed, and Poe kept few acquaintances from Richmond. He did, however, enjoy a brief reunion with his brother William, who lived in Baltimore. He lived with his Aunt Maria, and formed an intensely close relationship with the

older woman and her young daughter, Virginia. The Clemms'
extreme poverty bound them to Poe as they all struggled to
make ends meet. Later, it would be Poe's affection for young
Virginia that would turn the three into an actual family.

Poe's family had lived in the city for four generations, and
his grandfather was still remembered for his role during the
American Revolution. Poe found his relatives struggling to
get by. According to Silverman, his grandfather's widow was
"an elderly pensioner, partly paralyzed." His Aunt Maria was
even poorer, subsisting through sewing and dressmaking
and borrowing money from acquaintances. Like her brother,
Edgar's father, Maria was not afraid to "resort to the pity of
others" in order to survive. The death of Maria's husband,
William Clemm, shortly before Edgar arrived in Baltimore
had left Maria alone with her two young children, Virginia
and Henry. Poe moved in with the Clemms. Over time,
according to Meyers, Maria became a mother figure to him,
and was "absolutely devoted to Poe. She believed in his
genius, cared for him with a maternal solicitude and willingly
made great sacrifices on his behalf."

Poe's brother William was also living with Maria and her
children, which reunited the brothers for the longest period
since the death of their mother. Unlike Poe, who would later
embellish his biography with improbable journeys to Russia
and Greece, William had actually made several voyages
to the Mediterranean, South America, and possibly Russia
before he was twenty. Like his brother, William was a writer,
publishing approximately twenty stories and poems. While
Poe "borrowed" the details of his brother's life, William paid
tribute by naming the hero of one of his stories Edgar. Their
great affection for each other acknowledged the pain and
sympathy they shared through the loss of their parents.
Edgar once explained, " . . . It is not so much that they love

each other as that they both love the same parent—their affections are always running in the same direction—the same channel and cannot help mingling." However, the destructive drinking habits that pursued Poe's father and Edgar found William as well. Just six months after Edgar was reunited with his brother, William died—either of alcoholism or tuberculosis—on August 1. He was twenty-four, the same age as his mother when she had died.

It was during Poe's time in Baltimore that his relationship with John Allan also came to its sad conclusion. Although Allan had provided Poe with some money to pay debts, he had no substantial contact with his foster son. In April 1833, Poe wrote him one last letter. Instead of sharing his literary success, he emphasized his poverty. He pleaded with Allan to "save [him] from destruction." " . . . I am not idle—nor addicted to any vice—nor have I committed any offense against society which would render me deserving of so hard a fate." This was very much true. Although Poe had struggled with drinking and gambling, and would shortly resume that struggle in a short period in time, his years in Baltimore indicate he was sober and "industriously writing short stories and endeavoring to have them published." Allan did not respond, so in early 1834 Poe turned up at his former home in Richmond, where Allan lay seriously ill. Allan refused to see him. He died in late March without ever seeing his foster son. Allan's will, which provided for his illegitimate children, left nothing to Poe. It was a bitter end to a volatile relationship.

Over the next few years, Poe attempted to find work as a teacher and with local newspapers, largely without success. Unable to find a stable career, Poe lived in terrible poverty with the Clemms and tried to establish himself as a writer. In 1831, Poe had submitted five short stories to a contest sponsored by the *Philadelphia Saturday Courier*. Though he did not win, the judges were sufficiently impressed to run all five stories throughout 1832, marking Poe's first publication as a fiction writer. At twenty-two, according to Quinn, Poe's stories already demonstrated a "masterly suggestion of the supernatural, the preservation of suspense." Fortunately for Poe, Baltimore's publishing industry was flourishing. Between 1815 and 1833, 72 new publications were announced in the city. Though not all survived, it indicated an audience hungry for entertainment.

In 1832, the *Baltimore Saturday Visitor* ran an unusual notice. They had received several of Poe's manuscripts, and even though they did not print them, they wanted to give notice of an outstanding new writer: "We have read these tales every syllable, with the greatest pleasure, and for originality, richness of imagery and purity of style, few American authors in our opinion have produced any thing superior." A year later the *Baltimore Saturday Visitor* announced a contest to encourage literature: $50 for the best story and $25 for the best poem. Poe submitted one poem and six short stories. On October 12, 1833, Poe was announced as the winner of the short story contest for "MS [Manuscript] Found in a Bottle."

The tale is narrated as if it were a true story: a man survives a shipwreck only to be rescued by the ghostly crew of an enormous ship that is sucked in a whirlpool to the center of Antarctica. The narrator survives long enough to write his story and seal it in a bottle. Poe claimed—and one of the contest judges apparently later verified—that Poe also won the poetry contest but the judges chose not to award both prizes to one person. Of Poe's collection of stories, the judges wrote, "These tales are eminently distinguished by a wild,

John Pendleton Kennedy was one of the judges in a literature contest *put on by the* **Baltimore Saturday Visitor** *which Poe won in the* *short story division. The two became friends, and Kennedy would* *advise his writing career as well as helping out the destitute Poe* *when he could.*

vigorous and poetical imagination, a rich style, [and] a fertile invention."

Through the contest, Poe started a friendship with one of the judges, John Pendleton Kennedy. An author and lawyer who took a paternal interest in Poe, Kennedy advised him on which magazines to submit his stories to. He also gave the destitute writer clothes, food, and access to his horse. A year after Allan's death, Kennedy extended a dinner invitation to Poe, who admitted in a letter that he lacked the proper clothes and felt ashamed—and then asked Kennedy to loan him $20 for clothes. Poe had a lifelong habit of begging employers, friends and acquaintances for money, and later alienating them with his excessive behavior and public criticism. Kennedy, however, accepted Poe's eccentricities. The year Poe died, he described his old friend as "a bright but unsteady light [that] has been awfully quenched."

In 1835, Kennedy secured publication of four of Poe's stories for *The Southern Literary Messenger,* his most important contribution to Poe's career. Two of the stories, "Berenice" and "Morella," feature Poe's grim fascination with life after death. "Berenice" features one of Poe's many maddened narrators. In this instance, the narrator hates his wife but is obsessed with her teeth, believing they are somehow a cure for his insanity. In the end, he removes all of her teeth, and the gruesome operation kills her. The narrator of "Morella" is obsessed with his wife, whom he loathes. Morella dies in childbirth, and their daughter grows up to exactly resemble her mother. After the daughter falls sick and dies, the narrator brings her to the same tomb as his wife—and finds no trace of her. The story ends with his realization that his daughter was actually the reincarnation of his dead wife.

A third story, "Hans Pfaall," explores Poe's interest in hoaxes and tall tales told realistically. Now considered an early example of science fiction, "Hans Pfaall" tells the story of a bankrupt Dutch man who flees in a hot-air balloon to the moon to escape his creditors—perhaps a sly reference to Poe's financial difficulties. The story is rich with the details of how the balloon worked, the lunar landscape Hans encounters, and Poe's imagining of how to breathe in space.

Poe began working regularly for the *Messenger* and its editor, Thomas Willis White. He contributed critical reviews in addition to his short stories, and in the summer of 1835 White suggested that Poe join the *Messenger* staff in Richmond. In two letters to White, Poe expressed enthusiasm about returning to the city of his youth. The tone of the letters indicate Poe was desperate for some form of employment, and his diminished circumstances meant he would accept a less than decent paycheck. "I would gladly accept [employment], were the salary even the merest trifle," Poe wrote. " . . . For at present a very small portion of my time is employed." Ultimately, White offered $15 a week for his services. The literary opportunity also appealed to Poe. In an earlier letter to White, he noted, "To be appreciated you must be *read*."

It was, for the American people and aspiring writers, "the golden age of periodicals," as an Illinois magazine proclaimed. Between 1825 and 1850, the number of periodicals in American increased 600 percent; 4,000 to 5,000 new publications chased after money and readers. There were several reasons for the huge boom in reading materials:

Did you know...

When Poe moved to Baltimore, it was the third-largest city in America, with 80,000 residents. It was a city of "substantial wealth and general prosperity." An English visitor in 1835 remarked, "Baltimore is the handsomest place I have yet seen—here are the finest monuments—the prettiest girls and the cleanest City in the Union."

new printing technologies, a growing literacy rate, the low postage rate for newspapers, and a flourishing network of distribution. For the rest of his life, Poe would only work, when he was employed, for magazines. Despite the limitations of his job—long hours, meager pay, menial work—Poe was able to reach a wide audience with his short stories and poems. He also developed a reputation as a fierce, provocative critic, an aspect of Poe's life that will be explored later.

Poe's aesthetic theories, his strong beliefs on the qualities that make good poetry and literature he explored in the public eye as a magazine writer. In an 1845 essay, he summarized the impact the age or periodical had upon the writer, writing, "I will not be sure that men at present think more profoundly than half a century ago, but beyond question they think with more rapidity, with more skill, with more tact, with more of method . . . . Besides all this, they have a vast increase in the thinking material; they have more facts, more to think about ."

Remarkably, he was the only major American writer of his era to subsist entirely through his published work. Ralph Waldo Emerson was a minister; Henry Wadsworth Longfellow—with whom Poe launched a spectacular literary feud—was a teacher and had a wealthy wife; and James Fennimore Cooper, Washington Irving, and Nathaniel Hawthorne all had jobs outside the United States. The relative comfort of his peers deeply embittered Poe as his fame rose but his income did not. However, Poe's unfortunate situation gave his magazine writing vitality, as he was required to investigate "whatever was current and fashionable." From December 1835 to August 1836, Poe wrote 94 pieces for the *Messenger* covering "balloon flights, daguerreotypes, phrenology . . . shipwrecks, hidden treasure, epidemics, detection, murder [and] premature burial." His series, *Autography*, purported to discuss "how handwriting revealed character."

But it was not all fads and dubious science. Poe also covered poetry, philosophy, travel, and law. The amount of work he had to produce was prodigious. The classical education he received as a boy served him well, but Poe felt compelled to spend long hours at city libraries, along with borrowing books from friends. However, Poe sometimes found it necessary to use his imagination instead of facts. According to Myers, he was fond of "making up quotations and attributing them to famous authors, and inventing the titles of obscure volumes to give his work a scholarly tone."

Poe moved by himself to Richmond in the summer of 1835. No doubt it was difficult to return to the city where he had been rejected by his family and Elmira Royster. Thomas White had a fatherly concern for Poe, as well as admiration for Poe's "intelligence, talent and editorial skill," according to Myers. The two would ultimately clash over Poe's drinking—which renewed in earnest while in Richmond—and Poe's savage attacks on literature he deemed unworthy.

How Poe's relationship with fifteen-year-old Virginia Clemm developed is not certain. By the time he left Baltimore, he had developed romantic feelings for his young cousin. After a few weeks in Richmond, Poe was deeply dismayed to learn that another cousin, Neilson Poe, had taken pity on the destitute Clemms. Neilson wanted, as Myers puts it, to become "Virginia's guardian, to educate her, to provide a comfortable life, to introduce her to polite society." Most likely, Neilson also knew of Poe's connection with Virginia and disapproved. Poe's anguish was absolute. He wrote to Maria at the end of August, begging her to reject Neilson's offer. His letter opened, "I am blinded with tears while writing this letter." He continued, " . . . [I would take pride] in making you both comfortable & in calling her my wife. — But the dream is over. O God have mercy on me. What have to live for? Among strangers with not one soul to love me." Poe included a note to Virginia that ended, "[My] darling little wifey, think well before you break the heart of your cousin."

After establishing an accepting and nurturing family in Baltimore, Poe was overwhelmed at the thought of losing them. When Poe did not immediately hear from Maria, he fell into a deep depression and started drinking. The drinking made him increasingly unreliable, and in the fall of 1835, he either quit or was fired by White.

Poe returned to Baltimore to plead his case to Maria and Virginia. What happened between the three is not known, but Poe returned to Richmond in October with Virginia and Maria, and he married his cousin in 1836, although some accounts indicate that they married during his return to Baltimore. Although such a marriage would be illegal now, marriage between first cousins was not unusual in Poe's era. However, Virginia was a very young bride, even by the standards of the day. As much as Poe was in love with his wife, Silverman suspects that he was also in love with the idea of "both a wife and a mother, and perhaps . . . the symbolic value of restoring his original family." Virginia's middle name, ironically, was Eliza. Although Poe's actual sister, Rosalie, lived in Richmond, she had not developed mentally past the age of twelve, and was considered a plain, odd woman that Poe did not care to spend time around.

Until the end of his life, Virginia and Maria were Poe's devoted family. In turn, he lavished what little means he had on his young bride, who was described as "very plump" and "small for her age," with a "gentleness and simplicity." He instructed her "in every elegant accomplishment at this

Virginia Eliza Clemm. Although marriage between cousins was not unusual for that time, Virginia's age — fifteen at the time she married Poe — was considered even then to be too young for marriage.

expense . . . [and] became her tutor at another time," one of Poe's colleagues at the *Messenger* noted. "I remember once finding him engaged . . . in giving Virginia lessons in Algebra."

While still in Baltimore Poe wrote to Thomas White and asked for his job back. White was concerned about Poe's wild behavior when he was drinking but was genuinely fond of Poe and admitted in a letter that, "I was attached to you—and am still." He agreed to give Poe his job back, but vowed to immediately fire him if he started drinking. White sternly told Poe, "No man is safe who drinks before breakfast! No man can do so, and attend to business properly." Poe returned to Richmond in early October with Maria and Virginia and began their new life in a boardinghouse. The presence of his wife and mother-in-law soothed Poe's temper and restored his optimism: "My health is better than for years past, my mind fully occupied, my pecuniary [financial] difficulties have vanished. I have a fair prospect of future success—in a word all is right."

Poe published two new stories in the *Messenger*, "King Pest" and "Shadow—A Fable," and reprinted his wedding night horror story, "Loss of Breath." His work at the *Messenger*, however, established Poe as an incisive, sometimes deadly critic. With few writer friends, and no ties to America's literary establishment, Poe was free to express his frank opinions. Poe always hungered for recognition and was not afraid to attack others to get it. He savaged one book saying, "The most remarkable feature in this production is the bad paper on which it is printed." He wittily said of another book, "*The Swiss Heiress* should be read by all who have nothing better to do." Poe made his first literary enemies when he attacked the best-selling novel, *Norman Leslie*, by a New York lawyer named Leslie Fay. Poe disparaged Fay's writing style as "unworthy of a school-boy." The attack led Fay's friends to attack Poe in print for years to come. Despite the enmity Poe provoked, he was considered "one of the best editors of his time," according to Myers. Not even his enemies could deny his wit and talent. During his tenure at the *Messenger*, Poe published serious essays, including the first of several definitions of poetry.

As was the pattern throughout Poe's life, he would accept a responsibility or obligation and then chafe against its restrictions. Although circulation of the *Messenger* under Poe increased from 500 to 3,500, Poe still received the same low salary. Depressed over his situation, Poe started drinking again. By all accounts, Poe was an uncontrollable drinker and once he began, "he was unable to stop until he ran out of money or fell into a stupor." Even worse, Poe needed only a very moderate amount of alcohol to fly into a frenzy. A fastidious, polite man when sober, the drunk Poe was "coarse and vulgar." He admitted that he did not drink for pleasure but rather "to escape from torturing memories, from a sense of insupportable loneliness, and a dread of some strange impending doom." Whenever Poe could not bear his emotions any longer, he turned to alcohol. Rumors of his wild behavior when drunk circulated throughout the literary world, and Poe's enemies used it against him for the rest of his life and even thereafter. Every employer of Poe's complained about his drinking binges, and one nervous drinking spree prevented him from receiving a stable job with the federal government.

In late 1836, tensions between White—who knew his employee was drinking again—and Poe came to a breaking point. Poe claimed he had been ill and was tired of receiving such low pay for his demanding job. White was tired of having to defend his talented but often out-of-control employee and was under stress from other difficulties, including his wife's illness. He offered to keep Poe as a contributor, but he relieved him of his editorial position. Poe and his family stayed in Richmond until early 1837, when they departed for New York. Although Poe was now a writer with a growing national reputation, he was once again on his own.

Poe moved from New York and settled in Philadelphia, residing at this home at 530 North 7th Street from 1842 through 1844. While in Philadelphia, Poe would write such stories as "The Murders in the Rue Morgue."

4

In the Greenest of Our Valleys

AFTER LEAVING RICHMOND, Poe moved his family to New York and then to Philadelphia, where they lived for the next six years. Here, Poe would write his most famous and accomplished stories, publish his only novel, and achieve notoriety and respect as the editor of two magazines. With his story "The Murders in the Rue Morgue," Poe invented the modern detective tale. He established admiring relationships with fellow writers Charles Dickens and Nathaniel Hawthorne. Although Poe rarely rose above poverty, his home life with Virginia and Maria was largely happy and content.

Yet Poe's grip on security was tenuous as always. Four years after moving to Philadelphia, Virginia fell ill with tuberculosis. That same year, he quit or was fired from his job. He also made an important literary enemy, Rufus Griswold, the biographer who would slander Poe after his death. Several of Poe's triumphs still lay ahead of him, including "The Raven," but he would never again achieve the stability of his early years in Philadelphia.

There is little biographical detail of Poe's time in New York, and by summer 1838, the family had settled in Philadelphia. Shortly after moving, a New York publisher printed Poe's only novel, *The Narrative of Arthur Gordon Pym*. Much of the book, which details the disastrous sea voyage of the title character, was written in Richmond. Poe wove in numerous allusions to his life. Two different characters named Allan are executed; another character has the same initials of Poe's father and grandfather. Pym's closest friend is killed on the same date as William Poe.

Poe's novel received approximately two dozen reviews, some of them very favorable. The *New Yorker* proclaimed, "Those who delight in the wonderful and horrible have a feast before them." However, the attention to detail and description that made his short stories brilliant dragged down the narrative of a novel. Other critics reacted against the "disgusting" details, which included "a mutiny and atrocious butchery." After *Pym*, Poe abandoned his longer pieces, instead concentrating on a cohesive "unity of effect" that could be better sustained in shorter works.

At the time Poe moved to Philadelphia, it was losing its prominence among American cities. It still maintained a proud heritage, quiet atmosphere and "remarkably clean" neighborhoods. A visitor to Poe's house reported his "shabby-genteel appearance, his charming demeanor and his domestic tranquility." Poe was always considered a handsome man, with a large head, thick, dark hair and "full, brilliant eyes." He almost always wore a cheap black suit that he was careful to keep clean. Virginia was said to possess an "air of refinement and good breeding, and Mrs. Clemm had more of the mother than the mother-in-law about her." The family moved a handful of times, and one residence had a large enough garden that Poe almost bought a pet fawn to entertain Virginia.

The City of Brotherly Love witnessed the birth of Poe's greatest short stories. Unlike his poetry, with its tributes to idealized pasts and beautiful dead women, Poe's short stories "plunge into sadism and violence," and according to Myers, his characters are swept into "irrational states of consciousness—dreams, visions, swoons, stupors, fevers, fainting, epilepsy, melancholia, intoxication, claustrophobia, and hallucination." Poe's style had its origins in the Gothic tradition. According to Silverman, Gothic stories used "motifs of enclosure, premature burial, animated portraits and tapestries, putrescence and physical decay . . . [and] the use of mirrors, interior décor, and external landscape to reflect psychological states." Poe was careful to make his character's madness believable. Actions shocking to the reader made sense because of the character's frame of mind. In Poe's day, mental illness was barely understood. With no modern medicines or treatment for mental illness, those who crossed the line into insanity were not expected to return. As such, Poe's stories tapped a vein of psychological dread for many readers, while others were turned off by his grotesque, shameful descriptions.

One of Poe's first great short stories, "Ligeia," was published in September 1838 by a Baltimore magazine. He is thought to have received $10 as payment. In "Ligeia," the dead wife takes possession of her husband's second wife, Rowena, while Rowena is on her deathbed. The husband watches in amazement as the fair-haired Rowena struggles to revive herself while appearing to take on the physical appearance of his dark-haired first wife. Ligeia's rebirth dramatizes one of Poe's great themes, "how those most deeply beloved live on within oneself, never dead and ever ready to return." The story ends:

> And now slowly opened the eyes of the figure which stood before me. "Here then, at least," I shrieked aloud, "can I never-can I never be mistaken-these are the full, and the black, and the wild eyes-of my lost love-of the Lady-of the Lady Ligeia."

Poe found his first steady income in Philadelphia at *Burton's Gentleman's Magazine,* owned by William Burton, an actor and theater manager. Interestingly, *Burton's* had given the *The Narrative of Arthur Gordon Pym* its one entirely negative review. Poe needed work, though, and so he accepted Burton's offer of editorial work in the summer 1839. Poe contributed the same odd mixture of writing as he had at the *Messenger*. Articles reviewing gymnastic equipment ran alongside scathing attacks on celebrated writers such as Washington Irving and Henry Wadsworth Longfellow.

Poe lived during the Industrial Revolution, which sped America's transformation from an agricultural society to an industrial one. Poe's stories grapple with society's version of progress, about which he had mixed feelings. His stories largely take place in an unspecified past; his characters ride horses instead of trains and steamboats. Yet Poe's magazine work shows that he reviewed modern gadgets and inventions,

William Evans Burton owned the magazine Burton's Gentleman's Magazine, *which had actually given one of Poe's stories a bad review. However, Burton offered an editorial position to Poe, and since he needed the work, Poe accepted and began writing on a wide variety of subjects.*

and his stories of balloon travel indicate a fascination with machinery. In "The Man Who Was Used Up," which Poe contributed to *Burton's* in August 1839, the main character is a general who lavishes praise on modern inventions. The narrator, however, ultimately discovers that the general has lost nearly all of his original body parts in battle and wears prosthetic limbs and fake body parts held together by screws. Poe is clearly mocking society's "progress" by creating a barely human general as its mouthpiece.

The next month, *Burton's* published what is Poe's short-story masterpiece, "The Fall of the House of Usher." One of Poe's great contributions to literature was his introduction of poetic elements to fiction. In "Usher," the repetition of sounds, as well as "the abundance of dashes and other pauses, [creates] a mood of somber menace." The opening sentence survives its length and astonishing amount of detail because of Poe's innate sense of rhythm:

> During the whole of a dull, dark, and soundless day in the autumn of the year, when the clouds hung oppressively low in the heavens, I had been passing alone, on horseback, through a singularly dreary tract of country, and at length found myself, as the shades of evening drew on, within view of the melancholy House of Usher.

The gloomy house where the story takes place symbolizes the collapsing lives of its two residents, Roderick and his sister Madeline, the last of the Usher line. Poe's alliteration and his constant repetition of words—"upon" is used six times in one sentence—drives the narration. The appealing rhythm pulls the reader in, much as the narrator is seduced by the ruined, yet hypnotizing, features of the House of Usher. Madeline, who is wasting away from an unknown illness, soon dies, and Roderick begins losing his mind. At the end of the story Madeline reappears, having clawed her way out of the tomb where she was buried alive. Roderick reveals that he knew Madeline was alive when she was entombed and then dies of fright. As the narrator flees, the house—itself symbolic of madness—collapses and disappears into the ground.

"The Fall of the House of Usher" received high praise and helped cement Poe's reputation as a gifted writer. Two months later, a Philadelphia publisher brought out Poe's first widely reviewed collection of short stories, *Tales of the Grotesque and Arabesque*. Poe's general bad luck with money continued; instead of payment, he was given 20 free copies. The *New York Mirror* called the book "the development of a great intellectual capacity, with a power for vivid description, an opulence of imagination, a fecundity of invention, and a command over the elegances of diction which have seldom been displayed." However, the collection did not sell well. Perhaps the public was not ready to be pushed to "the full boundaries of the grotesque," as the *Philadelphia Saturday Courier* characterized the collection.

Did you know...

"The Philosophy of Furniture," Poe's contribution to interior design, continued his enthusiasm for wide-ranging subjects. Furniture should follow simple aesthetic guidelines, Poe wrote, and that money often corrupted good taste. He states in one passage, "With formal furniture, curtains are out of place; and an extensive volume of drapery of any kind is, under any circumstance, irreconcilable with good taste."

Poe continued working at *Burton's*, but the relationship between him and William Burton was becoming greatly strained. Poe resented his low pay and demanding hours while Burton disapproved of Poe's attacks on popular writers. The events that led to Poe's dismissal in May or June 1840 are unclear, but it seems Burton wanted to sell his magazine, which led Poe to announce his own long-simmering desire to own a magazine. In retaliation, Burton fired Poe.

Poe immediately started drumming up support and subscribers for his own magazine to be called *Penn*. In Poe's mind, his own magazine could provide the artistic and financial solution to his frustrations. According to J. Gerald Kennedy, independence "would enable Poe to combine his diverse talents as critic, tale writer, and poet into a single package. . . . [He] believed that a magazine would grant him the creative freedom that he had been denied by publishers and proprietors." However, by the winter of 1840 Poe was bedridden with a serious but unknown illness that delayed the project. More bad luck followed in early 1841 when a financial crisis sparked in Philadelphia forced local banks to suspend payment. With no money, Poe did not abandon the dream of his magazine, but meanwhile he began searching elsewhere for work.

His former employer, William Burton, sold his magazine to George Graham, a Philadelphia lawyer and publisher. Graham had admired Poe's plans for *Penn* and thought highly of his talents. In 1841, Graham hired Poe as an assistant editor for an annual salary of $800—$300 more than he had received with Burton and his richest salary to date. Graham relieved Poe of the drudgework, leaving him to write book reviews and contribute a story each month. Poe's ideas for a literary magazine were allowed to flourish; according to Myers, his "innovative tales, rigorous reviews, original ideas, good taste and literary contacts soon made *Graham's Magazine* the most important and astonishingly successful magazine in America." From a circulation of 5,000 the month Poe started, the magazine was printing 40,000 copies a year later. George Graham's ownership was much more liberal than other publishers of the day. He insisted on previously unpublished contributions, and he established a payscale for writers, common now but unheard of in Poe's era.

Poe the writer made an immediate impression. In April 1841, *Graham's* printed "The Murders in the Rue Morgue," which gave birth to the detective/crime genre. Although it is difficult to imagine now, there was no precedent for a tale that began with a crime that could be solved through logic and luck by the end. The novelty of such a story caused the *Pennsylvania Inquirer* to call Poe "a man of genius." They gushed, "At every step it whets the curiosity of the reader, until the interest is heightened to a point from which the mind shrinks with something like incredulity; when with an inventive power and skill, of which we know no parallel, he reconciles every difficulty." Poe, who was content to explore the same themes, was always looking for new techniques. Since he decided the outcome in advance in order to write the story, he knew the effect of the detective's analytical skills was "illusory." The trick of his detective story was that it had been written backward.

That same month, Poe met Rufus Griswold, a fellow writer and editor almost as sensitive and easily angered as Poe. Griswold's talent was vastly inferior to Poe's, but he had tremendous drive and gained great influence as the editor of a series of highly popular poetry anthologies. For this reason, Poe, who could grovel for favor as easily as he could attack, tried to ingratiate himself with Griswold.

Rufus Griswold was a writer and editor who had edited numerous poetry anthologies. While he was not as great a writer as Poe, he became his greatest nemesis. Griswold would even go so far as to publish a slanderous biography of Poe after his death.

Griswold did the same because he desired Poe's praise and critical acceptance. Although Poe was included in the anthology, he privately scorned it as "a most outrageous humbug." The animosity between them increased when George Graham hired Griswold at a higher salary than Poe. Poe later criticized the poetry anthology and Griswold in a series of public speeches. Griswold in turn privately disparaged Poe's name to fellow writers. Although both periodically attempted to charm the other for their own gain, the true relationship between the two men was usually competitive and hostile.

Although *Graham's* was hugely successful and allowed Poe further recognition as a writer and critic, he felt increasingly dissatisfied with his position. In a review of a Charles Dickens novel, Poe could have been referring to himself when he wrote, "[The] man of genius must write in obedience to his impulses. When forced to disobey them; when constrained, by fetters of a methodical duty . . . it is but a condition of his intellect—that he should occasionally grovel in platitudes of the most pitiable description." Frustrated and disgusted with his treatment, he resigned in April 1842 after about thirteen months.

Poe's unhappiness had a far deeper cause. In January 1842, Virginia was singing, a pastime she and Poe both enjoyed, when she began bleeding from the mouth. She was hemorrhaging from her lungs—a sign of tuberculosis. For two weeks she lay near death. Visitors found Poe "sensitive and irritable," and he would not allow anyone to consider Virginia's death, as "the mention of it drove him wild." Poe loved his wife very much—she embodied the "spirit of beauty" that he extolled in his poetry. George Graham visited the sad house and observed the effect Virginia's illness was having on Poe:

> The remembrance of his watchful eyes eagerly bent upon the slightest change of hue in that loved face, haunts me yet as a the memory of a sad strain. It was the hourly anticipation of her loss that made him a sad and thoughtful man, and lent a mournful melody to his undying song.

A few months after Virginia fell sick, *Graham's* published

one of Poe's great stories, "The Masque of the Red Death." Although Poe never said what inspired the story, it seems likely that Virginia's moribund state influenced the grim tale. A plague has swept through an unnamed country, killing everything in its path. The pestilence brings bloody death to its victims: "Blood was its Avatar and its seal—the redness and the horror of blood." Just as Virginia lay ill, helplessly coughing up blood, the victims of Poe's plague experience "sharp pains, and sudden dizziness, and then profuse bleeding." Just as Poe could not bear to face his wife's illness, the ruler of the land, Prince Prospero (Poe is spelled twice in his name), believes he can escape the plague by sealing his castle and entertaining his friends until the sickness passes. Death appears as a masked reveler, and Prospero dies as soon as he tries to attack him.

Poe's fortunes, along with Virginia's health, went up and down during their remaining two years in Philadelphia. After the first dangerous few weeks, Virginia seemed to recover her health, only to suffer another hemorrhage in June 1842. Virginia was just nineteen when she was struck with tuberculosis, which was in Poe's era "common, debilitating and dreaded." Her husband relied once again on drinking to ease his heartbreak. It is unclear how much Poe drank as his detractors often exaggerated his intake and his friends tried to shield him. But by 1843, according to Silverman, "his drinking was common knowledge around Philadelphia." One of the common myths about Poe is that he was an opium addict. In fact, there is no evidence to support that charge. Even one of Poe's enemies admitted, "I saw no signs of it and believe the charge to be baseless slander." It is likely he used opium in its medicinal form, laudanum, which in Poe's time was "dispensed almost as freely as aspirin is today," according to David Galloway.

In 1842, English author Charles Dickens undertook an American tour. Poe arranged to meet with Dickens, and Poe asked Dickens if he could help him find a publisher for Poe's work in England.

Meeting Charles Dickens proved to be one of the few bright spots during the first year of Virginia's illness. According to Silverman, Dickens was "the most famous writer in the English-speaking world" at the time of his 1842 American tour. In Philadelphia, a newspaper announcement that Dickens would shake hands for an hour brought a large mob to his hotel and the surrounding streets. Poe wrote to Dickens requesting a meeting, which Dickens agreed to. They had a long visit in early March, and the two great writers discussed the state of American poetry and Poe asked Dickens to use his influence in finding an English publisher for *Tales of the Grotesque and Arabesque*. Dickens agreed to help and later approached several English publishers, all of whom turned Poe down. Still, Dickens said he had a "pleasant recollection" of meeting with Poe and offered any future assistance to him.

Poe struggled for steady employment his last two years in Philadelphia. He announced his plans for a new journal to be called *Stylus*, but he could not find stable financial support. In his most disastrous attempt at employment, Poe applied for a job in the Philadelphia Custom House. There were several openings due to the new presidential administration of John Tyler, and a friend of Poe's with a government job assured Poe it was undemanding work with healthy pay. Poe was unable to get a job, so he decided to travel to Washington, D.C., and personally make his case to the president. According to Myers, while waiting in the capital for a mutual friend to make introductions, Poe, "nervous and excited, overeager and excessively convivial . . . got horribly drunk on port wine. . . . He went around with his coat turned inside out [and] became petulant." Poe was in no condition to meet the president, and his behavior shamed his friends.

Poe continued churning out stories that could not alleviate his poverty. In the three years after he left *Graham's*, he earned only $121 for his writing. Yet he was publishing some of his most famous stories, including "The Pit and the Pendulum" and "The Tell-Tale Heart," as well as "The

Mystery of Marie Roget," which brought back the popular detective-hero of "The Murders in the Rue Morgue," Auguste Dupin. In April 1844, Poe and his family moved to New York, where he thought he might find more success. In Philadelphia, Poe had consolidated his reputation as a master short-storyteller. Although he considered himself a poet first, according to Silverman, "his poetry remained little known and commented upon." That was about to change.

This portrait was published in Graham's Magazine *in February 1845 to accompany an article by James Russell Lowell about Poe. However, many, including Poe himself, found it to hardly resemble the subject. Nevertheless, this particular time period was one of the high points of Poe's literary career, as "The Raven" had been published in January 1845 in the* Evening Mirror.

5

Dearest My Life is Thine

IN APRIL 1844, Edgar and Virginia departed for New York City. At first, Poe was delighted to be in the city. In a letter to Maria Clemm, he enthused over their "nice chatty" landlady and the rich spread of food they enjoyed. Virginia was in "excellent spirits" although they both missed Maria and their cat, Catterina. Within a short time, however, he found the rough city "insufferably dirty," which was bad for Virginia's precarious health.

Poe's arrival in New York was humble, but he made his literary presence known six days later with a hoax published in the *New York Sun*. The headline—THE ATLANTIC OCEAN

CROSSED IN THREE DAYS!!—was Poe's outrageous account of flying across the ocean in a balloon. It is unclear how many people believed the hoax, but Poe described the *Sun* office as "besieged by people buying up copies."

Poe had announced his arrival, and quickly found a job at the *Evening Mirror*. His editorial skills had helped propel *Graham's* into the uppermost ranks of American magazines, but Poe was unable to build upon his success. The problem may have been Poe's reputation. His "peculiarities were known," writes biographer Hervey Allen. "If he were admired, he was also feared. There were few niches into which he would fit." According to Meyers, Poe's position at the *Mirror*, which earned $750 a year, required him to "sit at a desk, in a corner of the editorial room, ready to be called upon for any of the miscellaneous work of the moment—announcing news, condensing statements, answering correspondents, noticing amusements . . . ."

He also continued writing and publishing significant works, including "The Purloined Letter," the latest of Poe's detective stories, "The Premature Burial," and "The Oblong Box." He published the stories in 1844, a year before Texas became a state and the phrase "Manifest Destiny" defined the American philosophy of westward expansion. Poe's tales, popular as they were, were out of step with the spirit of exploration and self-reliance sweeping the country.

Meanwhile, Poe continued his psychological tales of what Silverman called "persons bricked up in walls, hidden under floorboards, or jammed in chimneys." In "The Oblong Box," the narrator is traveling on a ship with an artist who keeps an oblong box in his room. The narrator hears the artist open the lid every night, followed by quiet sobbing. He comes to believe the box holds a copy of Leonard Da Vinci's *Last Supper*. At the end, a storm batters the ship, and the passengers flee to lifeboats. The artist refuses to leave the box behind, and it is finally opened to reveal his wife, who had died the day the ship set sail.

The grief and tenderness the artist displayed toward his wife mirrored Poe's own feelings toward Virginia. The family, now joined by Maria, continued moving from place to place. In mid-summer 1844, they settled at the farm of Patrick Brennan. Poe had met the Brennans during one of his walks through the upper limits of the city. Today, Brennan's farm would be around Eighty-Fourth Street between Amsterdam Avenue and Broadway. When Poe discovered it, the farm extended from the Hudson River for 216 acres. According to Allen, Poe was "quite enchanted with the spot, the magnificent view, the excellent food, and the good nature of his hosts," and the family was happy to take in boarders. It was a happy time, "the last perfectly peaceful and happy hours that he was to know were passed under its roof. It still seemed possible, for those who could hope against hope, that in a place such as this Virginia might get well."

"The Raven" had taken shape while Poe lived in Philadelphia, but he finished it while living on the Brennan farm. One of the rooms supposedly contained a bust of Pallas, the Greek goddess of wisdom and war, whom Poe referred to in the poem. In his essay, "The Philosophy of Composition," Poe dramatized the construction of "The Raven." His wrote that his aim was to compose "a poem that would at once suit the popular and critical taste." He compared the challenge of constructing the perfect poem to solving a mathematical equation. He determined the perfect length to be roughly 100 lines—"The Raven" is 108 lines.

He chose the "death . . . of a beautiful woman" as his subject because it was "the most poetical topic in the world."

Needing a non-human creature to recite his refrain, Poe first picked a parrot, but then decided a raven was "infinitely more in keeping with the intended tone." The raven's constant refrain, "Nevermore," was perfect in its simplicity. The vagueness of the word is what drove the narrator mad, Poe said. His "intolerable sorrow" is shaken "by the melancholy character of the word itself, by its frequent repetition, and by a consideration of the ominous reputation of the fowl that uttered it."

There is still controversy over whether Poe did in fact write "The Raven" as he explained, or whether the essay is a tour of his techniques and theories but not a precise recollection of how his most famous poem was composed. Generally, it is considered an "idealized" account of the poem, regardless of whether Poe's writing process was, as Hayes puts it, "ultra-rational, the motive for the poem seems to be unreasoning sorrow." Poe's life was a series of unreasoning sorrows; his mother, Jane Stannard and Fanny Allan had all died at a young age, and his beloved wife was wasting away.

"The Raven" was published on January 29, 1845, in the *Evening Mirror*. It never made Poe wealthy but its popularity was instant. One reviewer described it as "one of the most felicitous specimens of unique rhyming which has for some time met our eyes." Another critic said, "In power and originality of versification the whole is no less remarkable than it is, psychologically, a wonder." The refrain was regularly quoted and even adapted into a play running in New York at the time. It was immediately the subject of numerous imitations, including "The Owl," "The Gazelle," and "The Pole-Cat," the last apparently admired by Abraham Lincoln. According to Myers, the poem was "printed throughout the country" and surpassed "the popularity of

An engraving from Poe's poem "The Raven." It became popular even at the time of its publishing, and met with much critical acclaim. Poe would give readings of the poem himself, and he was thrust into New York's elite literary society.

any previous American poem." At the end of 1845, a New York publisher printed a new Poe book to capitalize on his popularity, *The Raven and Other Tales*. Public fascination with Poe's grim bird made him a popular speaker, and according to Allen, the poem remained "his favorite for recitations on every occasion." One listener described Poe's method of arranging the mood to highlight his popular dramatic work:

> He would turn down the lamps till the room was almost dark and then standing in the center of the apartment he would recite those wonderful lines in the most melodious of voices . . . So marvelous was his power as a reader that the auditors would be afraid to draw breath lest the enchanted spell be broken.

Poe's sudden fame gave him entry into New York's literary society. According to Silverman, he was now invited to salons with "musicians, artists, poets, and myriad other people of talent, seeking an intellectual society where they could mingle for an evening and enjoy the advantages of money. . . . On the other side were gracious, intelligent, and usually affluent women (and some men)." The popular salon of Anne Charlotte Lynch, for instance, hosted Washington Irving, William Cullen Bryant, Ralph Waldo Emerson, and Herman Melville, and in 1845 and early 1846, Poe was a frequent visitor. Poe, raised with the manners of a polite Virginia gentleman, was ideally suited for the refined salons of the wealthy. Lynch described him as the perfect guest: "[He] had always the bearing and manners of a gentleman . . . interesting in conversation, but no monopolizing; polite and engaging."

Meyers writes that the women Poe encountered at the salons were "attracted to his creative genius, his prestige and power." These women were quite different from Virginia—they were more sophisticated and dedicated in their pursuit. For the rest of his life, he engaged in passionate but platonic relationships with these literary-minded women, often with the full knowledge of Virginia. Poe met the first of these women, Fanny Osgood, shortly after "The Raven" appeared. The married Osgood was immediately taken with Poe. Although her poetry was minor, he praised her in print, and the two composed poems to one another. One poem, called "To—" summed up Poe's attraction to Osgood but also his dedication to his wife:

> We both have found a life-long love
>> Wherein our weary souls may rest,
>
> Yet may we not, my gentle friend
>> Be each to each the second best?

While Poe enjoyed the attention and flattery of the literary women and exchanged many passionate letters and poems with them, his pursuit did not become more serious until later in life.

Poe's profile was raised a month after "The Raven" appeared when *Graham's* published a biographical essay by James Russell Lowell, a young poet. Lowell was perhaps the first to publicly suggest that Poe's place in literature was permanent: "[He] has attained an individual eminence in our literature, which he will keep." The two later fell out. Lowell accused Poe in print of lacking a moral conscience in his stories, but while they were still friends, he recommended Poe for a new magazine, *The Broadway Journal*. It was, according to Meyers, "more serious and intellectual" than any of Poe's previous magazines, which must have appealed to him. Although the pay was low, Poe was given a third of the magazine's profits each month, a potentially profitable arrangement.

Poe did not publish any major stories or poems in the *Journal*, but it was the scene of one of the bitterest public episodes of his career—his "war" with the poet Henry Wadsworth Longfellow. Poe had written to Longfellow in 1841, imploring him to write for *Graham's*. He praised Longfellow as "unquestionably the best poet in America." Longfellow, however, enjoyed a stable career at Harvard University and was married to a wealthy woman. His poetry also had a moralistic tone totally at odds with Poe's bloody tales. Poe, easily envious, privately resented Longfellow's good fortune and reputation. He accused Longfellow of plagiarizing a poem by Alfred Lord Tennyson, though no evidence existed. Poe's vicious attack continued with his review in April 1845 of Longfellow's latest book. The cruel review repeatedly dismissed Longfellow's poems as "exceedingly feeble," "singularly silly," "utterly worthless," "scarcely worth the page it occupies," and "We never saw a more sickening thing in a book."

For all of Poe's talents as a critic, the war on Longfellow was viewed by his colleagues a petty, personal attack. No doubt Longfellow represented everything Poe might have had access to had John Allan not disowned him. George Graham, Poe's former employer, exposed the likely source of Poe's envy in a letter to Longfellow: "I do not know what your crime may be in the eyes of Poe, but suppose it may be a better, and more widely established reputation. Or if you have wealth . . . that is sufficient to settle your damnation."

Poe's story "The Imp of the Perverse," published in the July 1845 issue of *Graham's* as the Longfellow war was dying down, was Poe's examination of the perversity of human impulse. It begins as a thoughtfully reasoned essay

Poe became embroiled in a public war of words with poet Henry Wadsworth Longfellow, constantly criticizing him and even accusing Longfellow of plagiarism. Many suspect Poe acted out of resentment and jealousy of Longfellow's wealth and position at Harvard University.

on how people are "propelled to act against their conscious desires," even when the consequences are totally destructive. In a twist only Poe could have imagined, the essay is eventually revealed to be a monologue by a condemned prisoner.

Poe's own such imp was rarely denied. This was never more evident than Poe's trip to Boston for a public speech in October 1845. Although he was a native son of Boston and his mother had encouraged him to remember it favorably, Poe was not fond of the city. Boston was home to the New England Transcendentalists, a group of writers, ministers, and teachers whose writings were concerned with "moral and ethical preoccupations." Ralph Waldo Emerson, the head of the transcendentalists, had dismissed "The Raven" with the comment "I see nothing in it."

Poe was highly dismissive of the transcendentalists and fashioned himself as an outsider in their midst. Poe's Boston audience was expecting the poet to read original work. For whatever reason, Poe failed to write any new pieces. Perversely, he chose to read one of his earlier poems, "Al Aaraaf," a long, confusing work. Much of the audience had left before Poe finally read "The Raven."

Boston critics rebuked his performance, and Poe retaliated with an editorial in *The Broadway Journal*. He claimed that he had read a boring poem on purpose: "It could scarcely be supposed that we would put ourselves to the trouble of composing for the Bostonians anything in the shape of an original poem. We did not. We had a poem . . . one quite as good as new. . . . That we gave them." He also suggested that he was drunk, which he was not.

Poe's life after "The Raven" was not marked entirely by literary brawls. He contributed important essays on the need for an international copyright law to the *Journal*. At the time, America had a copyright law, but British and European countries did not. This meant publishers were reluctant to pay American writers when they could publish British and European ones for free. Poe, always impoverished, was sensitive to this fact. Besides giving public support for a fair copyright law, he sought in his essays "a nationality of self-respect," which would begin with writers earning a decent wage. He believed American literature would greatly improve if it were open to the talented but poor writers instead of the mostly wealthy writers who could afford to pursue it.

Shortly after the disaster in Boston, Poe was on the verge of his lifelong dream—owning a magazine. In fact, it concluded as one of Poe's typically disastrous ventures. *The Broadway Journal* was struggling under debt, and Poe's relations with his editor were strained. So he formed an alliance with the *Journal's* third owner, John Bisco. After a whirlwind of deals, Bisco continued to publish the *Journal* with Poe as the sole editor, and according to Silverman, "receiving half the profits above the costs of publication." A month later, the *Journal*

Did you know...

An anonymous acquaintance, annoyed by Poe's continual criticism of Longfellow, published a letter in early 1845, defending Longfellow and accusing Poe of plagiarizing "The Raven." Poe responded with five letters over the next month defending his position and blasting Longfellow. In fact, the unknown letter-writer was most likely Poe himself. Longfellow had no idea who his defender was, even though he claimed to be a friend of the poet's, and his letter curiously calls Poe "one of our finest poets." Poe's bizarre exchange with himself failed to draw in Longfellow, who considered life "too precious to be wasted in street brawls."

was still in deep financial difficulty. Bisco quickly gave up and surrendered entire ownership to Poe. As Poe himself explained, "By a series of manoeuvres almost incomprehensible to myself, I have succeeded in getting rid, one by one, of all of my associates . . . [and] have now become sole editor and owner."

His confusion was justified. Within two days, he was begging people for loans, including Rufus Griswold. The issues that followed greatly strained Poe's abilities as he was forced to reprint his own work, publish mediocre work by his friends and overlook typographical errors. Poe, the critic who was once accused of "tomahawking" his enemies, breezily summed up such dull books as *The History of Silk, Cotton, Linen, Wool and other Fibrous Substances* as "able work." Unable to keep up with the demands of ownership, the magazine was shut down in January.

After the collapse of the *Journal*, Poe was often ill, and Virginia's own health was worsening. In March 1846, the family settled in Fordham, a village about 13 miles outside of New York City. Their little house was perched on a hill, with a porch and surrounded by cherry trees. The month before, Virginia had written her husband a Valentine's Day poem that began:

> Ever with thee I wish to roam—
> Dearest my life is thine.
> Give me a cottage for my home
> And a rich old cypress vine
> . . . Love alone shall guide us when we are there

The Fordham house was a respite for Virginia and a shelter from the humiliations and failure that followed Poe after "The Raven." "We three only lived for each other," Maria Clemm wrote later.

Virginia was rapidly deteriorating. One visitor to Fordham said, "When she coughed it was made certain that she was rapidly passing away." Poe's endless poverty barely afforded her any comfort. By November 1846, Virginia was near death, but she slept on a straw mattress with Poe's old military cloak as one of her few blankets. Adding to Poe's grief, according to Quinn, was "the bitterness of knowing that his poverty forbade him to even bring the great love of his life to an end in dignity and peace."

On December 15, the *New York Morning Express* ran an item informing readers of Poe and Virginia's illness and imploring friends to come to their aid. One of those who responded was Marie Louise Shew, a stranger to the Poes but a kind woman with "a heart for loving all the world." The daughter of a doctor, Shew had practical medical training to ease Virginia's last months. Shew visited often and provided as much care to Poe and Maria as she did to Virginia.

Virginia confided in Shew that she was concerned about her husband's welfare and wished him to carry on after her death. On January 29, she took a picture of Poe, kissed it and gave it to Shew. That night she was no longer able to speak and suffered great pain. Virginia Poe died the next day at age twenty-five and was buried near their cottage. Later that year Poe composed "Ulalume," his tribute to the undying presence of Virginia. The poem suggests the conflict between the living, who want to remain loyal to the dead while moving on with their lives, and the immortal love of the soul. At the end, the narrator surrenders to immortal love, realizing he will never forget the love of "thy lost Ulalume."

Elizabeth Fries Ellet was a poet who apparently fell in love with Poe after the death of Virginia. However, after the demise of their relationship, Ellet asked for her letters back, and sent her brother to retrieve them. This in turn led to Poe asking an acquaintance, Thomas Dunn English, for a pistol, but when English refused, Poe and English came to blows, and from then on the two attacked each other in print.

6

Out of Space, Out of Time

VIRGINIA'S DEATH WAS devastating to Poe. Her long decline had nearly driven him mad, and he drank to cope with the strain. A year after her death, he wrote in a letter: "I became insane, with long intervals of horrible sanity. . . . I drank—God only knows how often or how much. As a matter of course my enemies referred the insanity to the drink, rather than the drink to the insanity." Immediately after Virginia's death, Poe fell seriously ill, unable to cope with his loss. Echoing the actions of his grief-stricken characters, Poe would leave the house at night to visit his wife's grave.

The tangles of public life, however, intruded on his mourning.

The year before Virginia's death, Poe had struck up another literary friendship with a female poet, Elizabeth Ellet. According to Meyers, she reportedly "fell in love with, pursued and wrote emotional letters to [him]." After the relationship soured, Ellet demanded the letters she had written to Poe. He obliged, but unaware of this, she sent her brother to retrieve the letters. The brother, not believing Poe had returned the letters, threatened to kill him. Frightened, Poe visited Thomas Dunn English, the acquaintance who had once offered to introduce Poe to President Tyler, to ask for a pistol. After English refused and then insulted Poe, the poet punched English in the face, and a fistfight followed. By most accounts except for Poe's, English beat him badly.

After that unfortunate episode, the enmity between English and Poe hardened. They attacked each other in print, and English accused Poe of public drunkenness in the *Evening Mirror*. Unwilling to bear public humiliation, in July 1846 Poe sued English and the *Evening Mirror* for libel. The trial convened within two weeks of Virginia's death. English did not appear and no witnesses were provided. Poe won the suit and was awarded $225 in damages. While still locked in dispute with English, Poe published "The Cask of Amontillado," his great tale of revenge. The narrator of the story tricks a friend who has wronged him—although he never explains how—into visiting his extensive wine cellar, and then walls him up alive.

By the summer of 1847, Poe was once again appearing in public. He credited Louise Shew for giving him emotional strength and stability during the period after Virginia's death. At the beginning of 1848, according to Silverman, he "considered himself recovered not only from [Virginia's] death but also from the emotional riot that had preceded it." That summer, Poe began a series of romantic entanglements that consumed him until his death. Arguably, he knew that he would never love a woman as deeply as Virginia. Poe needed companionship, though, and he needed a woman to look after and inspire him.

The first of these women was a Massachusetts poet named Jane Locke. She had sent Poe a letter of condolence after Virginia's death, and the two began a correspondence. In July 1848, Locke arranged for Poe to speak near Locke's home in Lowell, Massachusetts. Their first meeting proved to be a disappointment. Locke was 45, married, and the mother of five children. His surprise led him to reject Locke's hospitality. Instead he stayed with her relatives, who lived nearby. There he met Nancy "Annie" Richmond, the wealthy wife of a paper manufacturer. Their attraction was instant. Richmond later described him as "incomparable." Unlike his literary friends, Annie was a "kind and simple lady." By Meyers' account, "Poe seemed to love her more deeply than any of the women he was involved with at the end of his life."

Annie, who was married and a mother, was unavailable as anything more than a friend. Poe began to court another woman, Sarah Helen Whitman. Whitman, a widow and a talented poet, lived with her mother and sister in Providence, Rhode Island. She became familiar with Poe through Fanny Osgood, who shared many details of her friendship with Poe. Whitman made her interest in Poe public with a poem written for Anne Lynch's Valentine's Day salon called "To Edgar A. Poe." Intrigued, he wrote her a reply called "To Helen." The last line read, "I dwell with Beauty which is Hope." On September 21, Poe visited her in Providence and set about trying to win her heart. In a letter he later wrote to Helen describing their first meeting, he rhapsodized, "Your hand rested within mine, and my whole soul shook with a tremulous ecstasy."

Although they had just met, he asked her to marry him. Helen asked for time to think. Poe continued pouring out his heart in letters while still maintaining an intense correspondence with Annie Richmond, who knew about Helen. His feelings for Helen were sincere but Poe was also practical. According to Silverman, he knew a marriage would "energize his literary ambitions and resuscitate his spirits."

After Poe returned to Fordham, Helen considered his proposal. Her friends, who included Rufus Griswold, warned her about Poe's drinking binges and his eccentric behavior. Also, unlike a youthful Virginia, Helen was too cautious and refined to consider adapting to Poe's poverty-stricken lifestyle. Yet she cared for Poe and was "unwilling to say the word which might separate us forever." Their emotional reunion ended with a "conditional" engagement and Poe's promise to swear off alcohol. Yet both were bound by too many doubts. Poe was unable to stop drinking and he was still declaring his love to Annie Richmond in letters. In December 1848, Poe and Helen met one last time. She knew he had continued drinking, and he despaired of earning her trust and quieting her doubts. Without it ever being said, when he left the next day both understood that the engagement was off.

Poe turned to Annie for comfort, but that relationship was also subsiding. Jane Locke, jealous of Poe's love for Annie, spread rumors about his relationship with Helen, and according to Meyers, "turned Annie's tolerant and deferential husband against Poe by distorting the nature of Poe's spiritual love for his wife." Poe's tribute to his beloved friend was published in March 1849. In "For Annie," Poe described the calming effect her friendship had on him:

> The sickness—the nausea—
> The pitiless pain—
> Have ceased, with the fever
> That maddened my brain

Nancy "Annie" Richmond and Poe were attracted to each other, but Richmond was married and had a family. While she was not part of the literary set, Poe was nonetheless drawn to her simple ways. However, he would continue to court other women while maintaining correspondence with Richmond.

Poe's creative output slowed during his emotional entanglements, but he did make some important artistic statements in the last year of his life. In May, he finished "Annabel Lee," which was not published until the month he died. The ballad once again addresses the spirit of undying love. The lyrical, sing-song rhythm belies the poem's tragic tone, which ends with the narrator sleeping on the tomb of his dead love. It is unclear to whom Poe addressed "Annabel Lee"—Annie, Helen and Virginia were all candidates. It is also possible that the idealized bride represented Poe's vision "of all the women he loved and lost."

At the end of 1848, Poe published what Meyers calls "one of his most important aesthetic statements, 'The Poetic Principle.'" The meaning and definition of poetry is a subject Poe returned to several times during his life. In "The Poetic Principle," Poe argued that poetry should not be used as a tool to advance moral, religious, or social beliefs. He believed that poetry could not flourish unless it existed for its own sake—that the true poet should pursue the medium and not the message. The greatest poetry, Poe suggested, is a glimpse of the divine that people are otherwise too preoccupied to see or feel. Meyers writes that these ideas, controversial at the time, were "the foundation of serious criticism in America. His ideas on brevity, originality, and unity of effect . . . his insistence upon the values of sound and rhythm."

Despite the spectacular failure of *The Broadway Journal*, Poe still nursed dreams of a literary magazine. He named the new enterprise *Stylus*. Although he continued selling work, Poe was otherwise unemployed, and according to Meyers, he hoped his own magazine "would provide a desperately needed outlet for his own work." Poe decided on a fund-raising tour of the South to raise support for his magazine. He arrived back in Richmond during the hot July of 1849. At first Poe had some tentative success. In August, E. N. H. Patterson agreed to subsidize a journal if Poe could find 1,000 subscribers. They agreed to meet in St. Louis on October 15. Poe also gave a lecture on "The Poetic Principle" in Richmond that was well reviewed by the local papers.

That summer Poe also renewed his friendship with Elmira Royster Shelton, his childhood sweetheart. Elmira was now a wealthy widow and mother of two children. The courtship appealed to both, as they had once been in love, and now were, according to Quinn, "clutching at the memories of youth, as youth was slipping away from them." Poe, never one to wait, proposed to Elmira in July, but she asked for time to think about it. Despite his reply that, according to Meyers, "a love that hesitated was not a love for him," Elmira insisted on seriously contemplating the proposal.

Like all of Poe's romantic relationships after Virginia, there were obstacles. Both of Elmira's children were opposed to the marriage and made fun of Poe behind his back when he visited the Shelton house. Her husband's will also stipulated that she would lose most of his estate if she remarried. However, according to Silverman, "by the end of August, rumors circulated in Richmond that Poe and Elmira Shelton were to be married." Despite her doubts, Elmira was attracted to Poe, whom she described as fascinating. To secure Elmira's trust, Poe joined a temperance society in late August and vowed to give up alcohol. After Poe's death, Elmira suggested that she and Poe were never engaged. However, she wrote letters to Maria Clemm, who kept a devoted correspondence with Poe, suggesting how dear Poe was to her:

> I am fully prepared to love you, and I do sincerely hope that our spirits may be congenial. There shall be nothing wanting on my part to make them so. I have just spent a very happy evening with your dear Edgar, and I know it will be gratifying to you, to know, that he is all that you could desire him to be, sober, temperate, moral & much beloved.

Poe also wrote to Maria in September, informing her of the planned marriage and asking her opinion on where the three of them should live. Poe suggested Lowell, Massachusetts, which indicates that he might have wished to be closer to Annie Richmond. In late September as the wedding was being planned, Poe planned a short trip to Philadelphia. A local piano manufacturer had offered Poe $100 to edit a volume of his wife's poetry. Always

Elmira Royster Shelton was a childhood sweetheart of Poe's, and in the summer of 1849, Poe renewed his friendship with her. He proposed to her in July, but Shelton was hesitant, and both of her children were opposed to the marriage.

needing money, Poe took the job. After Philadelphia, he would travel to New York for Maria and to settle his affairs before the wedding.

The night before Poe departed, he complained of a fever. Elmira suggested he delay his trip, but the next morning Poe left on a steamer for Baltimore. It was the last time she saw him. Silverman writes that Poe was not seen again until October 3, when he was discovered "at Gunner's Hall, a Baltimore tavern, strangely dressed and semiconscious." He was clearly drunk and possibly suffered from exposure to the strong winds and rain that had been lashing Baltimore. Poe managed to ask the young printer who had recognized him to contact Joseph Snodgrass, a longtime friend of Poe's and a Baltimore physician. When Snodgrass arrived at Gunner's Hall, he found the normally fastidious and articulate Poe wearing "a look of vacant stupidity. He wore neither vest nor tie, his dingy trousers fit badly, his shirt was crumpled, his cheap hat soiled." Snodgrass "thought he must be wearing castoff clothing, having been robbed or cheated of his own."

Poe was taken to the Washington College Hospital, where he remained unconscious until the next day. His cousin, Neilson Poe, who had long ago angered Poe, brought fresh sheets but was unable to visit him. Once Poe regained consciousness, according to Allen, he "was unable to tell Dr. Moran, the attending physician, how he had come to the condition in which he was found." Poe was confused and incoherent. He referred to a wife, possibly Virginia or Elmira. Moran tried to calm Poe, telling him he would soon recover and his friends would be able to visit him. Meyers writes that Poe's retort, "that the best thing his best friend could do would be to blow out his brains with a pistol," indicated the depth of his despair.

Poe lapsed into a delirium that continued until Saturday, October 6. At some point that night, he began to call loudly for "Reynolds." The identity of Reynolds is not certain, but one possibility is Jeremiah Reynolds, an explorer whose adventures Poe used as a basis for *The Narrative of Arthur Gordon Pym*. "Pym" ended with the narrator being sucked into a watery black hole, and at the end of the chasm he perceives a shrouded human figure waiting for him. It is impossible to know what struggles Poe imagined in the last days of his life, but if he was in fact staring into the black hole of eternity, he may have believed Reynolds was that ghostly figure at the end.

Poe continued calling for Reynolds until 3 A.M., Sunday morning, October 7. At that point, Moran recalled, "his condition changed. Feeble from his exertions he seemed to rest a short time." At 5 A.M. Poe suddenly exclaimed, "Lord help my poor Soul!" and died. He was forty.

Much of Poe's death is still a mystery. Dr. Snodgrass believed Poe had died from "a lethal amount of alcohol." Dr. Moran, however, attributed his death to encephalitis, "a brain inflammation brought on by exposure." Baltimore was experiencing wintry weather, and Poe was found without his own clothing. He had also had a fever when he left Richmond. Both doctors might have been correct; if Poe was totally intoxicated, he might not have cared about protecting himself from the elements. The location where Poe was found might have provided a clue to his death. Baltimore's Election Day was October 3, and Gunner's Hall, where Poe was found, was a polling place. At the time it was not uncommon for drunks to be grabbed by thugs working for politicians and forced to vote over and over, then abandoned once they had served their purpose. Poe's location makes that possibility intriguing, but there is no hard evidence. None of the newspapers of the time reported any trouble at the polls.

Poe took the truth of the last days of his life to the grave. The date of his burial is even uncertain; it was either October 8 or 9 and on a "raw and cloudy" day, according to Silverman. He was buried without Elmira, Maria Clemm, or any of his friends in attendance. Maria only learned of Poe's death the day of the funeral and had to write to Neilson Poe for details. Only four mourners attended the brief funeral, held at the Presbyterian Cemetery. They included Neilson Poe, Poe's uncle, Dr. Joseph Snodgrass, and a friend from the University of Virginia. By all accounts it was a minor ending. After a lifetime of separation from his family, Poe was interred in the family plot near his grandfather and brother.

Did you know...

There are other, more sinister, theories about his death. One recent biography of Poe purported to uncover proof that Elmira Shelton's brothers had, in fact, killed Poe. Elmira's family was unhappy about the marriage, and her three brothers may have wanted to protect the family name and money from an alcoholic poet with a scandalous reputation as a womanizer. In this version of Poe's final days, he did take the train to Philadelphia, where the brothers had followed him. They trapped him in his hotel room and insisted he continue on to New York, threatening his life if he returned to Richmond. Once his captors let him loose, Poe exchanged his usual clothing for an odd assortment of ill-fitting clothing and disappeared into Philadelphia for a few days. His plan was to quietly return to Richmond and inform Elmira of what happened. The Shelton brothers, however, had followed Poe, and when he got off in Baltimore, they were waiting for him. Knowing that sobriety was Elmira's main condition for marriage, they might have overpowered Poe and forced him to drink. Once he started drinking, writes biographer John Evangelist Walsh, they could abandon him knowing "he'd go on drinking until he was paralyzed . . . [and] likely would attract attention by causing some havoc."

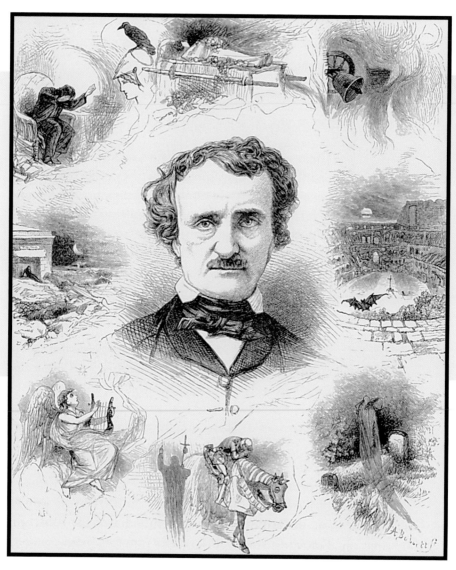

After his death, Rufus Griswold published a scathing obituary that claimed that "Few will be grieved by [his death], because he had few or no friends." However, Griswold's attempt to besmirch Poe's name only added to his legend.

7

In Sunshine and In Shadow

EVEN IN DEATH, Poe's life held one more strange twist. Two days after his death, Rufus Griswold, Poe's longtime adversary, published a vicious obituary in the *New York Daily Tribune*. "Few will be grieved by [his death]," Griswold write, "because he had few or no friends." He continued with an outright fabrication about Poe's mental health, "[He] walked the streets, in madness or melancholy, with lips moving indistinct curses."

Griswold's smear campaign was just getting started. Jealous of Poe's talents and sometimes a romantic competitor for the affections of Fanny Osgood, Griswold purposely set up to defame his rival's reputation and talents. Rosalie Poe should have been the heir to Poe's literary estate, but she was a humble, slow-witted woman. Maria Clemm was able to take control of her son-in-law's fortune. Griswold, knowing Clemm was in dire financial straits, approached her. He asked to be given control of Poe's literary estate. In return, Clemm would profit from editions of Poe's writings that Griswold published. With Poe's legacy in his hands, Griswold published memoirs that proved to be highly damaging. He alleged that Poe was an opium addict, that he had an affair with the second wife of John Allan, and that he had deserted the army. His motivations, like one of Poe's own sinister characters, were those of "undying hatred," according to Meyers. Because Griswold was respected as a minister and an editor, his accounts "were considered authoritative, and those who challenged him were ignored."

For decades, Griswold's vilification of Poe succeeded in distorting the facts of his life. The next major biography of him, which attempted to correct Griswold's portrait, did not appear until 1880. In France, poet Charles Baudelaire's essays on Poe, first published in 1852, revealed how differently Poe was viewed in Europe and how greatly he was admired. Quinn writes that Poe's struggles made him a romantic hero living in "a vast cage of mediocrity." Poe's depression, his drinking, and his unhappiness were signs that he was misunderstood, Baudelaire wrote. "The harsh apprentice of genius," Poe was doomed to wander "with the feverish unrest of one who was to breathe the air of a purer world." Ironically, Meyers writes that Griswold's distortions arguably increased Poe's popularity, guaranteeing that his "wicked and scandalous behavior . . . would continue to attract attention."

In fact, a number of Poe's friends, many of them women,

defended Poe against Griswold's attacks. In their eyes, his "utter refinement and unfailing chivalry" eclipsed his flaws. His friends had not forgotten that Poe the man was also an original artist. The French writer Paul Valery reminded his audience in 1930 that Poe "should be the inventor of several different varieties, should have offered the first and most striking example of the scientific tale . . . of the novel of criminal investigation, of the introduction into literature of morbid psychological states."

His influence on modern writers is striking. Oscar Wilde, James Joyce, Joseph Conrad, Eugene O'Neill, Vladimir Nabakov, Arthur Conan Doyle, Rudyard Kipling, Tom Wolfe, and F. Scott Fitzgerald all acknowledged their debt to Poe. His compelling exploration of psychological themes makes him unique among writers of his era and is one of the reasons Poe continues to resonate with modern audiences. One critic said of Poe, "[He] is the transitional figure in modern literature because he discovered our great subject, the disintegration of personality."

Poe never indicated that his stories were autobiographical. In "The Philosophy of Composition" he describes his approach to writing poetry as almost mathematical. It would be an insult to his gift of imagination to assume that Poe was documenting his life through short stories and poetry. In fact, when employed, his day-to-day life was busy with the mundane details of an editor. Yet it is difficult to believe the tragic facts of his life did not influence the themes Meyers lists as "love, loss, grief, mourning, alienation, terror, revenge, murder, insanity, disease and death." Poe lost most of the women closest to him, often at the peak of their youth and beauty. His literary creations—Annabel Lee, Lenore, Helen, Ulalume, Ligeia, Madeline Usher, and Eleonora— all die young and beautiful. The men who loved them

The grave of Poe in Baltimore, which is now adorned with cognac and roses in tribute to the author. The circumstances around Poe's death may never be fully known, and there were only a handful of mourners at his funeral.

struggle to face life after death. Silverman writes that much of Poe's work can be read as a kind of "prolonged mourning" from which neither he nor his characters fully recover.

The unfairness of a world that took so much from him led Poe to his greatest stories of revenge and murder. Yet his characters meet the consequences of their actions in the most unimaginable ways. Either by accident or their own design, Poe's characters find themselves in situations terrifying for their lack of logic: a friend who walls them up alive, a talking bird, the ability of the dead to come back to life, and the presence of Death himself at a party. It was the near-constant presence of tragedy in Edgar Allan Poe's life that kept the dead so real to him; in turn it was his genius to voice the mute fears of the unknown. Silverman writes, "The continuing appeal of Poe's work is owing to their power to confirm once-real beliefs from which most people have never entirely freed themselves . . . that one can be devoured and annihilated, that the darkness is astir, that the dead in some form survive and return."

1809   Edgar Poe is born on January 19 in Boston to Eliza and David Poe; the family lives in Boston until summer 1809, when they move to New York.

1810   David Poe abandons his family and is never heard from again.

1811   Eliza Poe dies in Richmond, Virginia, on December 8, possibly of yellow fever; Poe and his siblings are split up, and he is taken in by a prominent Richmond merchant, John Allan, and his wife, Fanny.

1815–1820   Poe travels with the Allans to England where John Allan runs the London branch of his business; attends boarding school and excels in his demanding studies.

1820–1822   The Allans and Poe return to Richmond, where Poe continues his schooling; over the next few years, Poe writes his first poems and attempts to publish a book.

1823   Poe meets Jane Stannard, the wife of a classmate; Stannard dies a year later after a period of insanity.

1825   Poe befriends his Richmond neighbor, Elmira Royster; the two fall in love and become engaged.

1826   Poe attends the University of Virginia in Charlottesville to study ancient and modern languages.

1827   John Allan refuses to pay for Poe's schooling and he withdraws from the University of Virginia; leaves for Boston, where he publishes his first book of poetry, *Tamerlane and Other Poems*; enlists in the U.S. Army, where he remains for two years.

1829   Fanny Allan dies; Poe leaves the army; while waiting to attend West Point, Poe moves to Baltimore and publishes his second book of poetry, *Al Aaraaf, Tamerlane and Minor Poems*.

1830   Poe attends West Point, but has himself expelled the following year.

1831   Poe moves to Baltimore, where he lives with his brother, his aunt Maria and her daughter Virginia Clemm; William Henry Poe dies in August of alcohol-related causes.

1833   Poe wins the *Baltimore Saturday Visitor* writing contest for "MS Found in a Bottle," his first and only honor during his lifetime.

1834   John Allan dies without reconciling with Poe and leaves his foster son out of his will.

1835 Poe moves to Richmond to write for *The Southern Literary Messenger*; Virginia and Maria Clemm move to Richmond.

1836 Poe marries Virginia Clemm.

1837 Poe quits the *Messenger* and moves to New York; writes his only novel, *The Narrative of Arthur Gordon Pym*.

1838 Poe moves to Philadelphia with his family; publishes his first great short story, "Ligeia."

1839 Poe is hired by William Burton to edit *Burton's Gentleman's Magazine*; publishes "The Fall of the House of Usher" and *Tales of the Grotesque and Arabesque*.

1840 Poe is fired from *Burton's*.

1841 Poe takes an editing position at *Graham's Magazine* for $800, the highest salary he will ever earn; invents the detective story with "The Murders in the Rue Morgue."

1842 Virginia Poe diagnosed with tuberculosis and suffers her first hemorrhage; Poe quits *Graham's* and attempts to find a government job; publishes "The Masque of Red Death" and "The Pit and the Pendulum."

1844 Moves to New York; joins the staff of the *Evening Mirror*.

1845 Publishes "The Raven" to widespread acclaim and tremendous popularity; gives lectures and visits literary salons; briefly owns *The Broadway Journal* but sells it to pay off debts.

1846 Moves to Fordham, New York, because of Virginia's health; publishes "The Cask of Amontillado"; Virginia grows increasingly sick and Poe also falls ill.

1847 Virginia dies; Poe sues the *Evening Mirror* for libel after a fellow writer defames him, wins the case and is awarded $225 in damages; at the end of the year publishes "Ulalume," his tribute to Virginia.

1848 Poe courts two women and proposes to one, Sarah Helen Whitman, but Whitman breaks off the engagement.

1849 Poe composes "For Annie"; sells two of his final poems, "The Bells" and "Annabel Lee"; travels to Richmond and renews his relationship with Elmira Royster Shelton, proposing marriage to her; disembarks in Baltimore, and on October 3 is discovered drunk and sick from exposure; dies on October 7.

"THE RAVEN"

Poem about a mysterious raven that appears in the library of a man grieving his lost love. The bird's persistent cry of "Nevermore" drives the narrator insane with fear and misery.

"THE FALL OF THE HOUSE OF USHER"

Short story about the demise of a family. The narrator visits his boyhood friend Roderick, who behaves strangely and appears to be wasting away. Roderick's sister Madeline is very sick, and she soon dies. At the conclusion, Roderick admits he buried Madeline alive, who then escapes from her tomb and confronts Roderick, who dies of fright. The narrator escapes the house as it collapses around him.

"THE TELL-TALE HEART"

Short story about a man who kills an old man and hides him beneath the floorboards. The man goes insane, believing he can hear the old man's heart beating, and confesses to police in order to stop the terrible sound.

"THE MASQUE OF RED DEATH"

Short story about a horrible plague sweeping an unnamed country. The prince of the land secures himself in his castle with enough food and friends to survive the plague. At a decadent party, Death appears in costume. He kills the prince and everyone in the castle.

"THE MURDERS IN THE RUE MORGUE"

Short story about Auguste Dupin, a French detective revered for his powers of intellect and deduction. He is asked to solve the brutal murder of a woman and her daughter. After finding an animal hair on the woman, he deduces that the murderer was an escaped orangutan. He finds the animal's owner, who admits that he witnessed the crime.

"THE BLACK CAT"

Short story about a man who blinds his cat in a drunken rage. His hatred of the animal grows, and one day he attempts to kill the cat, but is stopped by his wife. In a rage, he kills his wife. He walls up his wife and the cat in the basement, but the cat's shrieks give their location away and the man is apprehended.

"THE CASK OF AMONTILLADO"

During a street festival, the narrator runs into an acquaintance, Fortunato. He loathes Fortunato although he never reveals why. The narrator convinces Fortunato to visit his extensive vaults, which include a cask of Amontillado, a rare type of sherry. The narrator leads Fortunato deep into his catacombs, promising the elusive sherry. The narrator chains Fortunato and walls him up alive in the vaults. He reveals at the end that his crime has never been discovered.

BOOKS

The Narrative of Arthur Gordon Pym (1838)

POEMS

"To Helen" (1831)

"Lenore" (1831)

"The Raven" (1845)

"Ulalume" (1847)

"Annabel Lee" (1849)

"The Bells" (1849)

"For Annie" (1849)

SHORT STORIES

"Ligeia" (1838)

"The Fall of the House of Usher" (1839)

"William Wilson" (1839)

"The Man of the Crowd" (1840)

"The Murders in the Rue Morgue" (1841)

"The Masque of Red Death" (1842)

"The Pit and the Pendulum" (1842)

"The Tell-Tale Heart" (1843)

"The Gold Bug" (1843)

"The Black Cat" (1843)

"The Purloined Letter" (1845)

"The Cask of Amontillado" (1846)

"Hop-Frog" (1850)

"The Oval Portrait" (1850)

"Elenora" (1850)

"The Mystery of Marie Roget" (1850)

"The Man Who Was Used Up" (1850)

RODERICK USHER, "THE FALL OF THE HOUSE OF USHER"

Along with his sister Madeline, Roderick is the last remaining Usher. Though he was once healthy, he is now a pale, sick man who shrinks from daylight and can barely eat food. Roderick loses his sanity over the course of the story and buries Madeline alive, but tells his friend, the narrator, that she is dead. At the end, Madeline frees herself from her tomb and upon seeing her, Roderick dies of fright.

THE RAVEN, "THE RAVEN"

Described as "stately," with a "grave and stern decorum," the raven perches in the narrator's library and refuses to leave. He answers every question with "Nevermore." The narrator, who is terrified of the bird, refers to it as "grim, ungainly, ghastly, gaunt and ominous." He begs the bird to leave, but by the end of the poem, it is still there.

AUGUSTE DUPIN, "THE MURDERS IN THE RUE MORGUE," "THE PURLOINED LETTER" AND "THE MYSTERY OF MARIE ROGET"

Dupin is a French detective gifted with unusual skills of analysis and ingenuity. He solves crimes through "scientific logic and artistic imagination." He comes from a rich family that has lost all of its money and remains secluded except when he is solving bizarre crimes. In "The Murders in the Rue Morgue" Dupin alone perceives that the red hair clutched by one of the victims is not human. Knowing orangutans have red hair, he is able to conclude that an animal committed the savage crime.

NARRATOR, "THE TELL-TALE HEART"

"Why will you say I'm mad?" the narrator asks the reader in the opening paragraph. Clearly, the narrator, who is plotting to kill an old man he lives with, is insane. He tries to convince the reader that his actions are so logical, so obvious, that only a sane man would commit them. His madness will not allow him to forget his deeds. After he kills the old man, he believes he can still hear the heart beating. Terrified and enraged, he confesses to the police, whom he believes are already aware of his crime.

ANNABEL LEE, "ANNABEL LEE"

She is described as a beautiful child who lives in a kingdom by the sea. She and the narrator "loved with a love that was more than love" The narrator suggests that they are married, or would have married. She falls sick and dies, and her family buries her in a tomb by the sea. The narrator haunts her grave and sleeps by her side every night.

DEATH, "THE MASQUE OF RED DEATH"

A peripheral character in most of Poe's work, Death becomes the leading character in this short story about a bloody plague sweeping an unnamed countryside. Hoping to thwart the disease, Prince Prospero invites 1,000 of his closest friends to his palace, where they are sealed in to await the end of the plague. Death appears at a party—"tall and gaunt, and shrouded from head to foot in the habiliments of the grave." His grim costume echoes the horrors of the plague: "His vesture was dabbled in blood—and his broad brow . . . was besprinkled with the scarlet horror." Death is there to punish Prospero and his guests for their arrogance—by killing all of them.

Allen, Hervey. *Israfel: The Life and Times of Edgar Allan Poe*. New York: Farrar & Rinehart, Inc., 1934.

Foye, Raymond, ed. *The Unknown Poe*. San Francisco: City Lights Books, 1980.

Galloway, David, ed. *The Fall of the House of Usher and Other Writings*. England: Penguin Books, 1986.

Hayes, Kevin J., ed. *The Cambridge Companion to Edgar Allan Poe*. Cambridge: Cambridge University Press, 2002.

Kennedy, J. Gerald. *A Historical Guide to Edgar Allan Poe*. Oxford: Oxford University Press, 2001.

Meyers, Jeffrey. *Edgar Allan Poe: His Life and Legacy*. New York: Cooper Square Press, 1992.

Quinn, Arthur Hobson. *Edgar Allan Poe: A Critical Biography*. Baltimore: The Johns Hopkins University Press, 1998.

Silverman, Kenneth. *Edgar A. Poe: Mournful and Never-ending Remembrance*. New York: HarperPerennial, 1991.

Walsh, John Evangelist. *Midnight Dreary: The Mysterious Death of Edgar Allan Poe*. New York: St. Martin's Minotaur, 2000.

BIOGRAPHY

Allen, Hervey. *Israfel: The Life and Times of Edgar Allan Poe*. New York: Farrar & Rinehart, Inc., 1934.

Ingram, John H. *Edgar Allan Poe: His Life, Letters and Opinions*. London: John Hogg, 1880.

Meyers, Jeffrey. *Edgar Allan Poe: His Life and Legacy*. New York: Cooper Square Press, 1992.

Quinn, Arthur Hobson. *Edgar Allan Poe: A Critical Biography*. Baltimore: The Johns Hopkins University Press, 1998.

Silverman, Kenneth. *Edgar A. Poe: Mournful and Never-ending Remembrance*. New York: HarperPerennial, 1991.

Thomas, Dwight and David K. Jackson. *The Poe Log: A Documentary Life of Edgar Allan Poe, 1809-1849*. Boston: GK Hall & Sons, 1987.

CRITICISM

Hayes, Kevin J., ed. *The Cambridge Companion to Edgar Allan Poe*. Cambridge: Cambridge University Press, 2002.

Hoffman, Daniel. *Poe Poe Poe Poe Poe Poe Poe*. Baton Rouge: Louisiana State University Press, 1998.

Kennedy, J. Gerald. *The Historical Guide to Edgar Allan Poe*. New York: Oxford University Press, 2001.

Quinn, Patrick. *The French Face of Edgar Allan Poe*. Carbondale: Southern Illinois University Press, 1954.

Silverman, Kenneth, ed. *New Essays on Poe's Major Tales*. New York: Cambridge University Press, 1993.

Whalen, Terence. *Edgar Allan Poe and the Masses: The Political Economy of Literature in Antebellum America*. Princeton: Princeton University Press, 1999.

MUSEUMS

Poe Museum
1914-16 E. Main Street
Richmond, VA 23223
http://www.PoeMuseum.org

Edgar Allan Poe House and Museum
203 North Amity Street
Baltimore, MD 21223
http://www.eapoe.org/balt/poehse.htm

Edgar Allan Poe Historical Site
532 North 7th Street
Philadelphia, PA 19123
http://www.nps.gov/edal/

Edgar Allan Poe Cottage
2640 Grand Concourse and East Kingsbridge Road
Bronx, NY 10458.
http://www.museumregister.com/US/NewYork/Bronx/
    Fordham/AboutPoeCottage.html

WEBSITES
The Edgar Allan Poe Society of Baltimore
    http://www.eapoe.org/
Edgar Allan Poe's House of Usher
    http://www.comnet.ca/~forrest/
The Poe Decoder
    http://www.poedecoder.com/
The Work of Edgar Allan Poe (1809–1849)
    http://bau2.uibk.ac.at/sg/poe/poe.html
A Poe Webliography
    http://newark.rutgers.edu/~ehrlich/poesites.html

page:

10: AP/Wide World Photos
19: Hulton Archives/Getty Images
22: Rare Book Department, The Free Library of Philadelphia
27: Courtesy of the Edgar Allan Poe Society of Baltimore, Inc.
36: ©David Muench/CORBIS
40: ©Hulton-Deutsch Collection/CORBIS
42: Courtesy of the Edgar Allan Poe Society of Baltimore, Inc.
47: Courtesy of the Edgar Allan Poe Society of Baltimore, Inc.
53: Courtesy of the Edgar Allan Poe Museum, Richmond, Virginia
56: ©Bettmann/CORBIS
61: Courtesy of the Edgar Allan Poe Society of Baltimore, Inc.

66: Courtesy of the Edgar Allan Poe Society of Baltimore, Inc.
69: Hierophant Collection
72: Courtesy of the Edgar Allan Poe Society of Baltimore, Inc.
77: ©Bettmann/CORBIS
81: Hierophant Collection
86: Courtesy of the Edgar Allan Poe Society of Baltimore, Inc.
91: Courtesy of the Edgar Allan Poe Society of Baltimore, Inc.
94: Courtesy of the Edgar Allan Poe Society of Baltimore, Inc.
98: Courtesy of the Edgar Allan Poe Society of Baltimore, Inc.
102: AP/Wide World Photos

Cover: The National Archives and Records Administration, NWDNS-111-4202

JENNIFER PELTAK graduated from Temple University with a degree in journalism. She was previously a reporter and editor with two newspapers in northern Virginia. She currently resides in Washington, D.C.